Using
BRAIN SCIENCE
To Make
Training Stick

Using

BRAIN SCIENCE

To Make
Training Stick

Six Learning Principles That Trump Traditional Teaching

Sharon Bowman

Using

BRAIN SCIENCE

To Make
Training Stick

Six Learning Principles That Trump Traditional Teaching

Sharon L. Bowman, M. A.

Published by: **Bowperson Publishing**
P.O. Box 564, Glenbrook, NV 89413
Phone: 775-749-5247 Fax: 775-749-1891
Website: www.Bowperson.com

The Six Trumps® is a registered trademark
of Bowperson Publishing and Training, Inc.

Printed in the United States of America.

Cover design and text layout by: Ad Graphics, Inc.
www.TheBookProducer.com

ISBN: 978-0-9656851-1-5

My deepest thanks
to the great
teachers and trainers
I've met,
and to the brain science authors
I've learned from.
You have been
the inspiration for this book.

Table Of Contents

The Six Trumps® **15**

Read This First! **17**
   About The Activity 18
   More Choices 18

PART ONE: About This Book **21**
   About This Book 23
   Why Brain Science? 23
   Simple Is Smart 25
   It's Not Your Title: It's What You Do 25
   Mark-Ups 26
   What You'll Get From This Book 26
   The Rest Of This Book In A Nutshell 28
   Suggestions For Success 28
   Deal The Cards And Play The Game 30

PART TWO: Choose Your Own Learning **31**
   Choose Your Own Learning 33
   Web Warm-Ups 34
   What Do You Already Know? Quick Write #1 35
   What Do You Want To Learn? Quick Write #2 36
   Learning Principle One: Movement Trumps Sitting 38
      What Would YOU Do? 38
      Movement Trumps Sitting 42
      Summary Statement: Quick Write #3 42
      Adding Learner Movement 44
      More On Movement Trumps Sitting 46
      Choose And Use 46
      What Have You Learned? Fact Or Fiction 47
   Body Breaks 49
   Learning Principle Two: Talking Trumps Listening 50
      What Would YOU Do? 50
      Highlight It 52
      Talking Trumps Listening 55
      More On Talking Trumps Listening 56

Choose And Use 56
What Have You Learned? Three-Card-Draw 57
Learning Principle Three: Images Trump Words 59
What Would YOU Do? 59
A Picture Is Worth 1,000 Words 62
Images Trump Words 68
Fill-In-The-Blanks 69
Adding More Images 70
More On Images Trump Words 72
Choose And Use 72
What Have You Learned? More Mark-Ups 73
Learning Principle Four: Writing Trumps Reading 75
What Would YOU Do? 75
The Power OF Paper 79
Building In Writing Time 80
Writing Trumps Reading 82
Data Hunt 83
More On Writing Trumps Reading 84
Choose And Use 84
What Have You Learned? Cross It Out 85
Learning Principle Five: Shorter Trumps Longer 87
What Would YOU Do? 87
Shorter Trumps Longer 90
Chunk Your Own Learning 91
Timing The Content Segments: Quick Write #4 92
More On Shorter Trumps Longer .93
Choose And Use 93
What Have You Learned? Check It Off 94
Learning Principle Six: Different Trumps Same 96
What Would YOU Do? 96
How Different Is It? 99
Different Trumps Same 101
Treasure Hunt 101
More On Different Trumps Same 103
Choose And Use 103
Treasure Hunt Extravaganza 104
What Have You Learned? Three-Card-Draw Revisited 106

Bringing It Home To What You Do 108
What Do You Want To Learn? Quick Write #2 Revisited 110
Web Warm-Ups Revisited 110
What Have You Learned? Cross It Out 111
Choose Your Own Learning: What Was It Like For YOU? 113

PART THREE: Six Learning Principles That Trump Traditional Teaching **115**
  The Six Trumps® 117
  Learning Principle One: Movement Trumps Sitting 119
    1. Movement Enhances Cognition 120
    2. Movement Boosts Memory 120
    3. Movement Keeps Learners Awake 121
    4. Movement Increases Energy 121
    The Bottom Line 121
    What's In It For You? 121
  Learning Principle Two: Talking Trumps Listening 123
    1. Talking Increases Retention 124
    2. Talking Builds Relationships 124
    3. Talking Creates Meta-Learning 125
    4. Talking Elicits Feedback 125
    5. Talking Enhances Self-Worth 126
    The Bottom Line 126
    What's In It For You? 126
  Learning Principle Three: Images Trump Words 127
    1. Images Are A Brain Turn-On 129
    2. Images Evoke Emotions 129
    3. Images Trigger Long-Term Memory 130
    4. Images Create Short Cuts 130
    The Bottom Line 130
    What's In It For You? 131
  Learning Principle Four: Writing Trumps Reading 132
    1. Writing Stimulates Memory 134
    2. Writing Is Kinesthetic 134
    3. Writing Is Visual-Spatial 134
    4. Writing Grabs Attention 134
    The Bottom Line 135

What's In It For You? 135
Learning Principle Five: Shorter Trumps Longer 136
   1. Learners Remain Alert 138
   2. Learners Stay Engaged 138
   3. Learning Becomes Collaborative 138
   4. You Polish Your Content 138
   The Bottom Line 139
   What's In It For You? 139
Learning Principle Six: Different Trumps Same 140
   1. The Brain Responds To Novelty 142
   2. The Brain Responds To Contrast 142
   3. The Brain Responds To Emotion 142
   4. The Brain Responds To Meaning 142
   The Bottom Line 143
   What's In It For You? 143
Counting Your Cards 144
What Did You Get From This Book? Benefits Revisited 146

PART FOUR: Putting The Principles To Work **149**
Getting Started 151
   Let Go Of Comfort 152
   Time For Confidence 152
   Engagement, Not Perfection 152
   Combine Them 152
   Use The Ten-Minute Rule 152
   Keep It Short 152
   Mix Them Up 152
   Group Management Signal 153
   The Right To Pass 153
   Use What Works 153
   The Bottom Line 153
   The Six Trumps® Revisited 154
Working The Principle: Movement Trumps Sitting 155
   Movement And The Ten-Minute Rule 155
   Combine Content And Movement 155
   Hand It Over 155
   Make It Fun 155

Five Activities That Put The Principle To Work 157
    1. **Body Breaks** 158
    2. **Walk And Talk** 161
    3. **Wall-Writing** 164
    4. **Review Relay** 168
    5. **Beat-The-Clock (moving version)** 172
Working The Principle: Talking Trumps Listening 175
    Stop Talking 175
    From Low-Risk To High-Risk 175
    From Small Group To Large Group 175
    Two Before You 176
    Make It Open-Ended 176
Five Activities That Put The Principle To Work 177
    1. **Turn And Talk** 178
    2. **Standing Survey** 181
    3. **Each Teach** 184
    4. **Talking Whip** 187
    5. **Beat-The-Clock (talking version)** 190
Working The Principle: Images Trump Words 192
    Pictures In Place Of Print 192
    Slash The Slides 192
    Images For Need-To-Know Concepts 192
    Take The Time 193
    Explore The Net 193
    Give It Away 193
Five Activities That Put The Principle To Work 195
    1. **Say It With Symbols** 196
    2. **Mental Metaphors** 199
    3. **Story Starters** 202
    4. **Memory Maps** 207
    5. **Beat-The-Clock (drawing version)** 210
Working The Principle: Writing Trumps Reading 213
    Your Silence Is Golden 213
    Give It Away Again 213
    Be Specific 214
    Blanks Are Beautiful 214
    Vary The Places, Spaces, And Times 214

Five Activities That Put The Principle To Work 216
    1. Mark-Ups 217
    2. Quick Writes 221
    3. Three-Card-Draw 224
    4. Fill-In-The-Blanks 228
    5. Beat-The-Clock (written version) 232
Working The Principle: Shorter Trumps Longer 235
    Time Your Talk 235
    Space Your Slides 235
    Check In With Learners 235
    Bracket The Content 236
    Need-To-Know Versus Nice-To-Know 236
Activities That Put The Principle To Work 237
Working The Principle: Different Trumps Same 238
    They're Not In School Anymore 238
    Surprise Them 238
    Mix Them Up 239
    Something Old, Something New 239
    It's For You, Too 239
Five Activities That Put The Principle To Work 240
    1. Dot-Voting 241
    2. Sculpt It 245
    3. Learner's Toolbox 249
    4. Looks Like, Sounds Like 253
    5. Rhythm, Rap, And Rhyme 256
Where To Go From Here 259

PART FIVE: Brain Science Resources 261
Using The Resources 263
The Six Trumps® Workshop 266
Branching Stories: The Tale Behind Choose Your Own Learning . .272
The Biologist And The Educator 275
Brain Science Books 277
More Book Resources 279
Brain Science Websites 282
Sharon's Books, Website, And Bio 285

The Six Trumps®

In terms of learning:

1. **Movement trumps sitting.**

2. **Talking trumps listening.**

3. **Images trump words.**

4. **Writing trumps reading.**

5. **Shorter trumps longer.**

6. **Different trumps same.**

For more information, inquire within.

Read This First!

This Is No Ordinary Book

*T*his is no ordinary book because you get to choose how you want *to learn*. For example, if you would like to do a simple brain activity right now (it's a metaphor for learning), continue reading. If you want to read *about* the activity, turn to the next page.

For this activity, add up the numbers below:

1 2 3 4 5 6 7 8 9 10

Now answer two questions:

1. What answer did you get?

2. More importantly, how did you get the answer? Did you:

   Add the numbers beginning on the left and ending on the right?

   Add the numbers beginning on the right and ending on the left?

   Group the numbers (1+2+3, 4+5+6, etc.) and then add the groups?

   Add by 10s (1+9, 2+8, etc.) and then include the extra 10 and the 5?

   "Fold the line" and add by 11s (1+10, 2+9, 3+8, 4+7, 5+6)? If you did this, you're in good company: German mathematician Carl Friedrich Gauss folded the line, and then quickly created an algorithm (formula) so that he could add long lines of sequenced numbers in a few seconds. He did that when he was seven years old.

About The Activity

The activity is a metaphor for learning because are many ways to learn and, for that matter, many ways to teach. Most of the time there isn't really a "right" way. However, some ways work better than others. Some ways increase your speed of learning and your ability to remember and use what you learned.

The activity also represents pattern-making. The human brain is a pattern-seeking organ. Its main job is to make sense out of the patterns it perceives, and then to create something meaningful from those patterns. You did this when you figured out a way to add the numbers. Maybe you added them the way you were taught to add. Maybe you thought, "There has to be a quicker way than this" and hunted for a different pattern. Maybe you instantly "saw" the groups of tens or elevens. Maybe the exercise wasn't meaningful to you at all and so you skipped it entirely.

Everyday you figure out patterns and make them meaningful in your own way. This is called learning. Of course, you already know this. What you might not realize is that, even when reading a book, you come to an understanding of the book's concepts in your own individual way that differs from what other readers might do.

For example, some people read chapter-by-chapter. Others skim pages for specific ideas they can use immediately. Some want the information first; application comes later. Others want stories like case studies, anecdotes, and reality-based scenarios. Still others want to learn by solving problems and discovering the book's concepts (patterns) for themselves.

More Choices

Because you get to choose how you want to learn, you will decide what you want to read first, in which order, and why. Here are your choices:

Part One: About This Book. If you like to begin at the beginning and get a bird's-eye view, so to speak, about the contents of this book, turn to page 21 and begin there.

Part Two: Choose Your Own Learning. If you like learning-by-doing and being actively involved the entire time while you answer questions and solve training-based challenges, turn to page 31 and begin there.

Part Three: Six Learning Principles that Trump Traditional Teaching. If you want to read the brain research with concepts and data presented in a logical, chapter-by-chapter format, turn to page 115.

Part Four: Putting the Principles To Work. If you decide to save the research for later reading, and just need some quick, brain-based activities you can use immediately, turn to page 149.

Part Five: Brain Science Resources. You might decide to skim the book titles, websites, and other resources upon which this book is based. If you want to do this first, turn to page 261.

Still More Choices. Of course, you can flip through the entire book until something grabs your interest. Or, you can mix it up and read different parts at different times for different reasons, all the while learning in a more random fashion.

The Bottom Line. All these approaches to this book will work, so choose how you want to learn, then enjoy your learning journey!

You must keep an open mind,
but not so open that your brains fall out.
James Oberg

PART ONE

About This Book

About This Book

*An interest in the brain requires no justification
other than a curiosity to know
why we are here, what we are doing here,
and where we are going.*

Paul MacLean

Why Brain Science?

The field of cognitive neuroscience studies how the human brain takes in, stores, retrieves, and uses information. This branch of science has exploded with information in the decade leading up to this book's publication. Not all the information is new; some concepts have been around for forty years or more. But cognitive scientists and educators are finding new ways to *apply* this information, and the need for *application* is greater than ever.

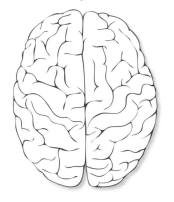

Because It's Logical. Those of us who train and teach for a living—who, in other words, work with the human brain every day—need to know as much as possible about how the human brain learns. How can we expect the people we teach to remember *what* we teach if we don't know *how* they learn it, or even *how* to teach it well?

Knowing the brain science that forms the foundation of effective instruction is like knowing the rules of the road. Could you drive without knowing any of the rules? Of course. Would you probably cause a host of driving problems for yourself and others (not to mention disasters of immense proportions)? Most certainly. The same applies to teaching others without knowing how the human brain learns. You can do it, but you increase the probability that it won't work well. And, the disasters can be significant for the learners.

It just makes sense.

Because It's Physical. Brain science also explains the hard-wiring of the human brain with respect to learning. Physiologically, the brain pays attention to certain things and ignores others. Much of these attention swings occur on a subconscious level. Knowing what makes or breaks attention, and what to do about it when teaching others, is crucial for successful instruction.

Furthermore, brain research indicates that physical movement improves cognitive performance. As facilitators of learning, our challenge is to find ways to weave learner movement into the fabric of the learning experience, without wasting valuable instruction time while doing it.

Because It's Emotional. For too long, there has been an assumption that traditional classroom instruction should be fact-based, that is, devoid of emotion. The standard has been to separate feelings from education. Now brain science proves otherwise: *everything* the human brain learns is filtered through emotions. No

exceptions. How we make use of emotions to enhance learning will determine how successful the learning is.

Simple Is Smart

I have laid out this book in an easy-to-read style and format, but the concepts are grounded in solid research. Obviously, the research I have chosen to cite is that which I feel is the most helpful *in terms of learning and teaching.* However, like most science, cognitive neuroscience is replete with books, journals, articles, and websites that often use complex scientific language to describe relatively simple concepts. I have translated these concepts into simple-to-remember phrases and descriptions so that you can use them more easily.

It's Not Your Title: It's What You Do

Trainer, teacher, instructor, facilitator, learning specialist. What you call yourself is *not* important. What you *do* is imminently important. Regardless of your job title, understanding more about brain science will help you become better at what you do.

In this book, I use the words teacher, trainer, and instructor interchangeably. Ditto for teaching, training, and instructing. Rather than debating vocabulary, ask yourself: "Can I use this information to make my instruction more effective?" If the answer is "yes," then incorporate the concepts and activities into your work. If the answer is "no," move on to other ideas in the book until you find ones that will be effective for you and your learners.

Mark-Ups

Before reading any further, take one minute to gather as many of the following materials as you can:

- ▶ A pen or pencil
- ▶ A highlighter
- ▶ A few colored markers
- ▶ Post-It® notes and Post-It® flags
- ▶ Some index cards

Put them all in a small tote or paper bag. Keep it with this book. As you read, you'll be using these materials to mark up this book: writing comments, crossing out phrases, circling, highlighting, and boxing sentences or paragraphs. You'll be writing on Post-It® notes and flagging important pages.

Marking up a book is an excellent way to remember printed material. It also helps you quickly find what you think is important.

Put This Activity To Work: Have a variety of writing and drawing materials available for your learners to use. Place an assortment of these items on each table for small groups. If the room has individual desks, put the materials in containers that learners can pass around. For more about *Mark-Ups*, turn to page 217.

What You'll Get From This Book

Grab a highlighter. Listed on the next page are the benefits you'll get from this book. Highlight the ones that are most important to *you*.

After working through this book, I will be able to:

1. *Apply* six learning principles that are based on current brain science about how humans learn best.

2. *Explain* to training colleagues, co-workers, family, and friends why the learning principles are important to know for anyone who makes a living instructing others.

3. *Involve* learners in quick, easy, fun, and memorable ways so that they remain actively engaged throughout the entire learning experience.

4. *Increase* learners' physical energy and enthusiasm, even during the delivery of complex, dry, or technical content.

5. *Add to* my own physical energy and enthusiasm when I teach.

6. *Adapt* many of the classroom strategies to online, self-study, or computer-based programs.

7. *Receive* learner evaluations that indicate high satisfaction with what they've learned and how they've learned it.

8. *Feel* my own satisfaction for a job well done.

9. *Access* supporting resources to enhance my own learning and to improve my teaching.

10. *Teach* others what I've learned so that they, too, can make the transition from traditional to brain-based instruction.

Use a Post-It® note to flag this list—we'll come back to it later.

This Rest Of This Book In A Nutshell

Below are more detailed descriptions of the parts of this book that follow.

Part Two: Choose Your Own Learning. Six learning principles are presented in a structured, self-paced, learn-by-doing format. You'll answer questions, solve challenges, and check your responses against mine. You'll apply all six principles even as you learn about them. Better yet, you'll be able to use the activities with your own learners.

Part Three: Six Learning Principles That Trump Traditional Teaching. This part covers the six principles in a more linear, chapter-by-chapter format. Each chapter defines and describes one principle and includes references from some of the best twenty-first century brain science resources.

Part Four: Putting The Principles To Work. This part contains practical strategies and activities for applying the principles. You can flip through Part Four to find the activities that will be the most useful for you and the most interesting for your learners. Use Post-It® flags to mark the activities you plan to use.

Part Five: Brain Science Resources. Here you'll find book titles, websites, articles, and more to deepen your understanding of brain science.

Suggestions For Success

Baby Steps. Don't change everything you are doing all at once. Instead, experiment with one or two activities from this book until you feel comfortable using them. Then add others. Be patient with yourself and

your learners; you are changing how you teach and how they learn. Change takes time.

Use What Works. Choose only the strategies that you think will work for you and your learners. You won't choose everything in this book and some activities will work better than others, given your environment, your learners, and your content. Use an activity a few times until you get a sense of how it works. Change it to make it work better or choose a different activity. There are enough activity variations in this book to make most readers happy with their choices.

You Are Not Your Learners. As I've already mentioned, people have different learning preferences. What works for you as a learner may not work for others. So be prepared to step out of your comfort zone as you experiment with new ways of training. And, by all means, give learners the brain science behind the activities so that they, too, understand the *why* behind the *how* and *what*.

Have Fun And Learn From It All. Endorphins (the pleasure chemicals in the brain) are powerful reinforcers of learning. The more your learners enjoy the entire learning process, the better they will feel about themselves and about learning in general.

The same can be said about you as the instructor. The more you enjoy your job, the better your teaching skills will become. And you just might find yourself having so much fun that that you'll want to do more of it: within your company or school, and with community, church, or non-profit groups. You might find yourself becoming the trainer everyone wants to learn from, the teacher-of-teachers, or the highest-rated instructor in your company or educational institution (wouldn't that be cool?).

Deal The Cards And Play The Game

 If you're familiar with card games, you know that the trump card or suit is the one that beats all the others. It's the best card or suit to have in the game. You win the game when you trump the other cards.

Playing cards is another useful metaphor for learning. The trump card represents a way of learning that beats other more traditional learning methods. When one learning strategy trumps another, it means that it is a better, more powerful way to learn than the other.

In each of the six learning principles in this book, one learning strategy trumps another:

1. Movement trumps sitting.   *4. Writing trumps reading.*

2. Talking trumps listening.   *5. Shorter trumps longer.*

3. Images trump words.   *6. Different trumps same.*

This book applies these principles to your reading experience. Especially in Part Two, you will use the principles even as you're learning about them.

Here is my favorite card-playing quotation, also printed in *Training from the BACK of the Room* (2009). It is a great learning and teaching metaphor:

> *Break the rules!*
> *Instead of beginning with the tedious task*
> *of explaining flush, royal flush, pairs,*
> *and so on, to teach poker,*
> *deal the cards and play the game.*
> Michael Allen

PART TWO

Choose Your Own Learning

Choose Your Own Learning

All learning IS experience.
Everything else is just information.
Albert Einstein

Welcome to a structured, self-paced, learn-by-doing experience!

During this part of the book, you will *explore* the brain science that trumps traditional teaching and *use* six learning principles even as you learn what the principles are. Better yet, you'll have many opportunities to apply the principles to realistic instructional situations.

If you create online or computer-based courses, you'll receive a special benefit because you'll learn how to design printed content that is both informative *and* interactive. Elearning guru and author Clark Aldrich, in his book *Learning by Doing* (2005), calls this type of interactive, printed material "branching stories." Simply put, a branching story is one where the story changes, depending upon the choices you make as you read the story. For more about branching stories, turn to page 272.

The same holds true for this *Choose Your Own Learning* experience. Your choices will determine how you proceed through the content. No two readers will proceed exactly the same way. And yet, in the end, you will have learned precisely what you were meant to learn.

Now turn the page and remember to have your mark-up materials handy.

Don't lose your head
To gain a minute;
You need your head –
Your brains are in it.
Burma Shave

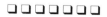

Web Warm-Ups

Right now, if you have five minutes and a computer with Internet access, consider doing one or both of the following *Web Warm-Ups*. These are Internet searches that will give you some pre-exposure to a few of this book's major concepts.

If you decide to skip the *Web Warm-Ups* for now (you can always come back to them later), turn to page 35 and continue reading.

1. Do an Internet search for one of the following phrases. Then skim the websites listed. For now, you don't have to click onto any of the websites unless you find something really compelling:

   ► Cognitive neuroscience and learning
   ► Cognitive science and learning
   ► Human brain and human learning
   ► TedTalks and brain science
   ► Brain-based learning
   ► Brain rules

2. Log onto www.amazon.com or www.youtube.com and explore the descriptions of the books and videos that have to do with the following:

   ► Brain rules
   ► Informal learning
   ► Brain science and human learning

Skim the title lists you find. Bookmark anything that sparks your interest.

You have just familiarized yourself with some of the language and phrases that are similar to the concepts you'll find in this book. Furthermore, you now know there is a wealth of information at your fingertips that you can explore later, if you wish.

Put This Activity To Work: With *Web Warm-Ups*, you encourage learners to begin exploring some general topic-related concepts on their own. Send the suggestions out via email, Internet or Intranet site, or flyer. Then, as an opening activity during the training, give learners a few minutes to share with others what they discovered in the *Web Warm-Ups*. You can find a variety of *Warm-Ups*, web-based and otherwise, in my book, *Training from the BACK of the Room* (2009).

❏ ❏ ❏ ❏ ❏ ❏ ❏

What Do You Already Know?
Quick Write #1

In the next ten seconds, think about what you already know about brain science and how humans learn. Then take another twenty seconds to jot down your thoughts in the brain below. Time yourself, and quit writing after half a minute is up.

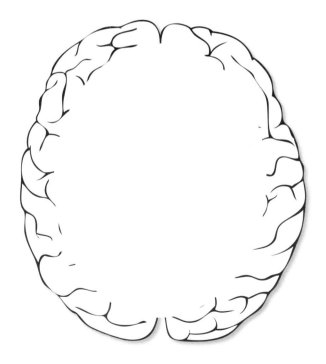

Put This Activity To Work: Tell learners do the *Quick Write* described above as an opening activity. Of course, you'll tailor the exercise to the topic you're teaching. For example, you might say:

> *Ask yourself what you already know about this topic. Then write one or two sentences describing what you know. Later, we'll come back to what you've written and compare it to what you have learned during the class.*

It only takes thirty to sixty seconds and by doing so, learners will be more able to link new concepts to prior knowledge. This will help them understand and remember the new content.

❏ ❏ ❏ ❏ ❏ ❏ ❏

What Do You Want To Learn?
Quick Write #2

On the banner below, write one learning outcome or personal goal describing something you want to be able to do after reading this book. Then flag this page with a Post-It® note; you'll be coming back to this *Quick Write* later.

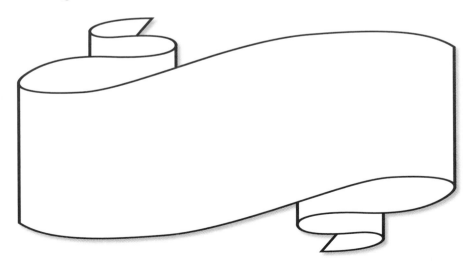

Put This Activity To Work: Suggest to learners that they think about what *they* want to learn, then write down their own learning goal. When they do this, they increase their interest in the topic and their willingness to learn more about it. Also, they will consider the content to be more relevant to their work and lives because they have identified personal reasons for learning.

My Notes

Learning Principle One:
Movement Trumps Sitting

What Would YOU Do?

You have a lot of intense content to cover that is very dry, technical, or complex. You will be lecturing most of the material, with much of the lecture information printed on PowerPoint® slides. You know this is not the most effective way to teach the content, but you have been directed to do it this way.

How do you plan to keep your learners awake and alert throughout the content delivery? Circle one answer below, then check your answer against mine by turning to the indicated page.

A. I plan to insert short, frequent, physical breaks into the instruction about every ten to twenty minutes. During each break, learners will spend a minute standing, stretching, and discussing the lecture content. *Turn to the top of page 39.*

B. I plan to lecture for about fifty minutes and then give learners a ten-minute break during which they can stand, stretch, and walk around. *Turn to the top of page 40.*

C. I plan to lecture for about ninety minutes, at which point learners will have a fifteen-minute break. I can't afford to give up any more time for breaks than that. *Turn to the bottom of page 40.*

A. I plan to insert short, frequent physical breaks into the instruction about every ten to twenty minutes. During each break, learners will spend a minute standing, stretching, and discussing the lecture content.

Yes, you just ensured that your learners will stay awake and alert because you took human physiology into account.

If you want to check how much more you already know about this first principle, continue reading. If you want to skip the following exercise for now, turn to page 42 and read the section *Movement Trumps Sitting*.

Draw a box around the following statements that are true and cross out the ones that are false:

1. Movement distracts learners from focusing on the content.

2. When learners move, oxygen to the brain increases, thereby enhancing both learning and memory.

3. Taking a scheduled ten-minute break once an hour is enough movement for most learners.

4. It becomes difficult for most learners to remain focused on content when they've been sitting and listening longer than about ten to twenty minutes.

5. Cognitive function increases when the human body moves and decreases when the body stays motionless too long.

Turn to page 41 for the answers.

B. I plan to lecture for about fifty minutes and then give learners a ten-minute break during which they can stand, stretch, and walk around.

Indeed, you can do this, and learners can certainly sit for fifty minutes. How much content they will remember is another matter. If they are involved in note-taking and small group discussions during the hour, learning will increase. If they're just sitting motionless and listening the whole time, without any engagement at all, the amount of learning will decrease. Go back to page 39 and read the correct answer.

C. I plan to lecture for about ninety minutes, at which point learners will have a fifteen-minute break. I can't afford to give up any more time for breaks than that.

You can't afford __not__ to. Sitting and listening to a ninety-minute lecture on complex data is a learning disaster. You need to engage them during the lecture so that they will remember the content. Go back to page 39 and read the correct answer.

On page 39 you drew a box around the statements that were true and crossed out the ones that were false. Check your responses against mine below.

1. ~~Movement distracts learners from focusing on the content.~~

2. When learners move, oxygen to the brain increases, thereby enhancing both learning and memory.

3. ~~Taking a scheduled ten-minute break once an hour is enough movement for most learners.~~

4. It becomes difficult for most learners to remain focused on content when they've been sitting and listening longer than about ten to twenty minutes.

5. Cognitive function increases when the human body moves and decreases when the body stays motionless too long.

Movement Trumps Sitting

This is the most important of the six learning principles covered in this book. Its importance has been overlooked ever since formal learning environments such as classrooms were first invented. Furthermore, even though most train-the-trainer and teacher education programs give lip service to the need for learner engagement, most learners still spend the majority of classroom time sitting. It's both physically and cognitively damaging for them to do so.

Molecular biologist and author John Medina, in his brilliant book *Brain Rules* (2008), makes a case for the importance of movement as it relates to cognitive function. The more physical movement we insert into our daily environments—in our classrooms, offices, meeting rooms, homes—the stronger we become, both physically and mentally. It naturally follows that people in classrooms learn better when they're given opportunities to move.

If you want to learn more about John Medina's research, do the following *Quick Write* exercise. If you want to skip this research for now, turn to page 44 and continue.

Summary Statement
Quick Write #3

Flip to pages 119-120 and read the first six paragraphs. After you've done this, come back to this page. In the balloon on the next page, write a short summary of what you learned from the information about Medina's research.

Put This Activity To Work: Instead of you giving a verbal summary of the content, have learners write short summary statements. If time allows, they can share their summaries with a partner or with their table group.

❑ ❑ ❑ ❑ ❑ ❑ ❑

Adding Learner Movement

Below are four common ways trainers move while teaching. On the lines after each scenario, write one way that learners could stand and move instead of, or in addition to, the trainer. Then compare your answers with mine.

A. The trainer walks to a flip chart and, as learners verbally state what they want to learn from the class, the trainer writes their statements on the chart paper.

_____

_____

_____

B. While standing, the trainer shows a slide with a list of learning objectives and then reads the list aloud to the learners.

_____

_____

_____

C. The trainer moves to the side of the room where information is posted on a flip chart. She points to the information while reading from the chart.

_____

_____

_____

D. While learners watch, the trainer uses hand gestures to demonstrate operating a machine.

_____

_____

_____

As long as your statements reflect some learner activity, your responses are better than what the scenarios describe. See if your responses are similar to the ones I've written below.

A. The trainer walks to a flip chart and, as learners verbally state what they want to learn from the program, the trainer writes their statements on the chart paper.

Learners write their own learning goals on Post-It® notes and then stand, walk to the flip chart, and stick their notes on the chart. Then they return to their seats.

B. While standing, the trainer shows a slide with a list of learning objectives and then reads the list aloud to the learners.

The trainer directs everyone to stand and form pairs or triads. Still standing, learners read the list of objectives aloud then tell their partner(s) which objective is the most important to them.

C. The trainer moves to the side of the room where information is posted on a flip chart. She points to the information while reading from the chart.

The trainer invites everyone to join her around the posted flip chart information. As the trainer lectures from the chart, she invites volunteers to read some of the information aloud. Then they all return to their seats.

D. While learners watch, the trainer uses hand gestures to demonstrate operating a machine.

Learners copy the trainer's movements.

More On Movement Trumps Sitting

When you have time, read the entire chapter in Part Three titled *Movement Trumps Sitting*. Use colored markers to circle, check off, or draw boxes around information that you consider important enough to remember. Multi-colored *Mark-Ups* are fun, different, and more visually noticeable than using the same color throughout. If you have questions or comments about the concepts, write them in the margins for later review.

Choose And Use

Below are the titles to five activities from Part Four that apply the principle *Movement Trumps Sitting*. Highlight the one that looks the most interesting to you, then turn to that page and flag it with a Post-It® note. Include this activity in your next training.

1. *Body Breaks (page 158)*

2. *Walk And Talk (page 161)*

3. *Wall-Writing (page 164)*

4. *Review Relay (page 168)*

5. *Beat-The-Clock (page 172)*

What Have You Learned?
Fact Or Fiction

In the margin, mark each of the following statements as *FACT* or *FICTION*. Then compare your answers with mine.

1. Physical exercise decreases cognitive performance.

2. It's very difficult to include physical exercise in classroom or online programs.

3. Movement, even just going from sitting to standing or from standing to walking, increases cognitive function.

4. A regularly scheduled, ten-minute break after fifty minutes of lecture is enough to keep learners' brains alert and active.

Here are my answers:

1. *FICTION.* Physical exercise decreases cognitive performance. *Brain science has now proven beyond doubt that physical movement enhances brain function.*

2. *FICTION.* It's very difficult to include physical exercise in work or learning environments. *It's actually easy to include standing, stretching, bending, and walking in a class or work environment when the movement only lasts for a few seconds or for one or two minutes.*

3. *FACT.* Movement, even just going from sitting to standing or from standing to walking, increases cognitive function. *As circulation increases, the brain receives more oxygen, thereby enhancing its ability to think and learn.*

4. *FICTION.* A regularly scheduled, ten-minute break after fifty minutes of lecture is enough to keep learners' brains alert and active. *On the contrary, learner movement needs to be part of the entire learning experience, especially during the lecture segments.*

Put This Activity To Work: Do a quick *Fact Or Fiction* review on paper, on slides, verbally, or by vote. For the latter, have the learners raise a hand if the given statement is a fact. Even better, learners stand if the statement is a fact and remain seated if it's fiction. Now you've added movement to the verbal *Fact Or Fiction* review.

Body Breaks

Read the next paragraph and then spend about sixty seconds doing what it describes:

Stand, stretch, and take a few deep breaths. If you wish, walk around the room. Or, walk down a hallway and back. If you're near an outside door, go outside, stretch and breathe deeply, then come back inside. As you do this, think about how you would explain to a colleague the first learning principle of this book.

Put This Activity To Work: Have learners take one-minute *Body Breaks* before, during, and after lecture segments and between the regularly scheduled breaks. They can stand, stretch, or walk around a chair, table, or the room.

Besides increasing blood circulation and oxygen to the brain, topic-related *Body Breaks* also enhance retention. Suggest to learners that they think about the content or talk about it with other learners while stretching or walking.

Can you apply *Body Breaks* to elearning? Of course. The *Movement Trumps Sitting* strategies and activities in Part Four will explain how.

Learning Principle Two:
Talking Trumps Listening

What Would YOU Do?

You are teaching concepts that are totally new to your learners. Because of this, it will be difficult for learners to *apply* the concepts until they *understand* them. Circle the statement below that describes the best course of action to take. Then check your answer against mine by turning to the indicated page.

A. I will lecture all the important information first. Then I will engage learners in a series of practice activities that apply the concepts. *Turn to the top of page 51.*

B. I will lecture all the important information *and* include quick *Body Breaks* between the lecture segments. During the *Body Breaks*, learners will talk about what they have learned so far. Then I will engage learners in a series of practice activities that apply the concepts. *Turn to the middle of page 51.*

A. I will lecture all the important information first. Then I will engage learners in a series of practice activities that apply the concepts.

Although this sounds logical, it isn't the best way to ensure that learners can remember and use the information later. A lot of relearning will have to take place during the practice activities. Read the correct answer below.

B. I will lecture all the important information *and* include quick *Body Breaks* between the lecture segments. During the *Body Breaks*, learners will talk about what they have learned so far. Then I will engage learners in a series of practice activities that apply the concepts.

This is the best course of action to take. Including <u>Body Breaks</u> during the lecture will help learners stay alert. If you have learners talk about the concepts while doing the <u>Body Breaks</u>, you've increased the odds not only that they'll remember the information but that they'll remember it for a longer period of time.

If you want to explore how much you already know about this learning principle, do the following exercise. Otherwise, turn to page 55.

Highlight It

Read the italicized, unfinished sentence and highlight the phrases below it that make the sentence correct. Then check your answers against mine.

When learners talk to each other about the content:

A. They deepen their own understanding of the material presented to them.

B. They confuse themselves with erroneous information.

C. They feel psychologically safer and more comfortable with each other as they learn.

D. They get distracted and learn less.

E. They process the information three times, thereby increasing their retention of it.

F. They quickly move on to other topics and away from the content.

G. They give each other verbal feedback, thereby acting as "teachers" as well as "learners."

Did you highlight the phrases listed below?

When learners talk to each other about the content:

A. They deepen their own understanding of the material presented to them.

   Yes, for most people, verbal processing leads to a better understanding of information versus just hearing it.

C. They feel psychologically safer and more comfortable with each other as they learn. *Again, yes.*

   The feelings of safety and comfort are crucial for optimum learning. Allowing learners to engage in short, topic-related discussions is one way to build emotional safety into a learning experience.

E. They process the information three times, thereby increasing their retention of it.

By processing three times, I mean that learners first hear the information when you present it, then they revisit the information twice more when they think about it and then put it in their own words.

G. They give each other verbal feedback, thereby acting as teachers as well as learners.

Absolutely. When learners give each other feedback as to whether or not the facts they are discussing are correct, they are teaching and thereby reinforcing the content in their own mind as well as their partner's.

What about phrases B, D, F?

B. They confuse themselves with erroneous information.

Actually, learner discussions help clarify content, and learners are more willing to ask questions if they are unsure of something.

D. They get distracted and learn less.

The opposite is true: they focus on the content and thus learn more.

F. They quickly move onto other topics and away from the content.

This only happens if the discussion time is too long. When discussions are kept short, learners will not have time to get off track.

Put This Activity To Work: Provide highlighters for use with printed material. Periodically throughout the lecture segments, tell learners to highlight certain phrases, sentences, or important concepts. Here are a few examples of what you might say:

▶ *Take a moment to find the main idea in this paragraph and highlight it.*

▶ *Think about what you just learned. Skim this page and highlight the information that supports the material we covered.*

▶ *Skim the six bulleted points on this page and highlight the one you think you're most likely to forget.*

▶ *Highlight the words or phrases that you want to remember.*

You can also create a multiple-choice quiz like the one you just took, and have learners highlight what they think the answers are. Then use the quiz as a pre/post activity.

Talking Trumps Listening

This is the second learning principle, and the easiest to combine with the other five. When you give learners short segments of time in which to discuss the content with each other, retention increases significantly. Even a minute or two of a partnered discussion after each lecture segment will be more beneficial to the learners than no discussion at all.

Of course, learners need to listen as well as talk. And because you are the instructor, you will be doing a considerable amount of talking. But take note: while you are talking, your learners may be actually *learning* less than you think they are. They are *hearing* you speak, but whether or not they will be able to remember and use all the information you've delivered is a different matter.

On the other hand, when given a minute or two to discuss what they've heard, learners immediately begin to process the information a second time. They deepen their understanding of it and can give each other feedback about the material. Additionally, they begin to move the content into long-term memory. Finally, they feel psychologically safer to form opinions and ask questions about the material.

❑ ❑ ❑ ❑ ❑ ❑ ❑

More On Talking Trumps Listening

When you have time, read the entire chapter in Part Three titled *Talking Trumps Listening*. This time, use colored markers to prioritize what you consider to be the most important concepts: red for need-to-know, yellow for useful, green for nice-to-know. By varying the ways in which you mark up printed material, you add visual interest and novelty to the activity.

Choose and Use

Below are the titles to five activities from Part Four that apply the principle *Talking Trumps Listening*. Highlight the one that looks the most interesting to you, then turn to that page and flag it with a Post-It® note. Use this activity the next time you teach.

1. *Turn And Talk (page 178)*

2. *Standing Survey (page 181)*

3. *Each Teach (page 184)*

4. *Talking Whip (page 187)*

5. *Beat-The-Clock (page 190)*

What Have You Learned?
Three-Card-Draw

Get three index cards. On the first, write "What?" On the second, write "So what?" On the third, write "Now what?" On each card respectively, write a short answer to the following three questions:

- **Card #1: What?** *What is one new idea you have gotten from this book so far?*

- **Card #2: So what?** *Why is this new idea important to you and the work you do?*

- **Card #3: Now what?** *What is one way you could use this idea when you teach?*

You will be writing again on your cards as you read this book, so be sure to put them with your writing materials or tuck them inside the book cover.

Put This Activity To Work: Pause periodically to give learners time to fill out their cards. They can write a number of answers to each specific question. They can use the backs of the cards as well, or add cards to their stacks. If time allows, have them share what they've written with a partner or with their table groups.

Other labels for the cards are: facts, opinions, questions, comments, major ideas, resources, procedures, summary statements, etc.

For more ways to use *Three-Card-Draw*, turn to page 224.

Learning Principle Three: Images Trump Words

What Would YOU Do?

You are presenting a rather rigorous company procedure for point-of-sale customer service. You have lots of return on investment statistics about what it costs your company when a customer is dissatisfied and leaves, versus the benefits and profits when a customer is satisfied and stays.

There are a number of ways to introduce this topic. Highlight the best introduction *in terms of learning* from the descriptions below. Then turn to the indicated page.

1. I would begin with a short verbal summary of the company's history and customer service goals. *Turn to the top of page 61.*

2. I would direct learners to spend a minute talking with a partner about a great customer service experience they had. *Turn to the top of page 60.*

3. I would begin by using slides to show the statistics regarding what the company gains or loses with good or poor customer service. *Turn to the bottom of page 61.*

4. I would begin by telling a real-life story about a great customer service experience that occurred within the company. I would add enough details to make the story interesting and emotionally compelling. *Turn to the middle of page 60.*

2. I would direct learners to spend a minute talking with a partner about a great customer service experience they had.

This is an excellent way to introduce this topic. It engages learners right from the start, connects them with the topic and each other, and helps them create a mental image of what great customer service looks like. In addition to this strategy, read answer #4, below.

4. I would begin by telling a real-life story about a great customer service experience that occurred within the company. I would add enough details to make the story interesting and emotionally compelling.

This is also an excellent way to introduce this topic (read answer #2 above). Telling a story creates mental images that stick when the facts may be forgotten. Images help learners remember new information in visual ways that statistics alone can't.

Regardless of the topic, storytelling creates image-rich content that is easily remembered. If you want to do another image-related exercise, turn to page 62.

If you want to skip ahead and read more information about this learning principle, turn to page 68.

1. I would begin with a short verbal summary of the company's history and customer service goals.

   While this may be important information to cover later, it's not the most compelling way to begin in terms of _learning_. Go back to page 60 and read the two answers there.

3. I would begin by using slides to show the statistics regarding what the company gains or loses with good or poor customer service.

   This information won't stick in learners' minds until they've made their own personal connections to the topic and until they've created a mental image to which they can connect the statistics. Go back to page 60 and read the two answers there.

A Picture Is Worth 1,000 Words

On the next few pages are a series of slides. Notice which ones grab your visual attention and are more interesting to look at. Also notice which ones you can more readily visualize after looking at the series.

1. **Movement Trumps Sitting**

- *Brain Rules* author John Medina says that "Exercise boosts brain power." Movement increases oxygen to the brain which enhances cognitive function.

- Movement that is done in short timed segments of a minute or less is still be beneficial to learners. Examples of short movement breaks in between longer scheduled class breaks are: stretching while sitting or standing, walking in place or around the room, and turning in their seats or standing and turning in order to discuss content with other learners.

- Teachers and trainers need to include more learner movement during the class or training. Learner movement should take place about every ten to twenty minutes between content delivery segments.

2. **Talking trumps listening.**

---

2. **Talking Trumps Listening**

- *Brain Matters* author Patricia Wolfe states: "The best way to learn something is to teach it." Learners begin to master what they are learning when they have time to teach it to someone else. This also increases long-term retention.

- Learners teaching learners can take many forms: paired or small group discussions, small group presentations to the class, paired or group skill demonstrations, dramatizations (also called role-plays), collaborative games and projects, self-correcting worksheets and tests.

- Teachers and trainers need to create ways for learners to teach each other and learn from one another throughout the learning experience.

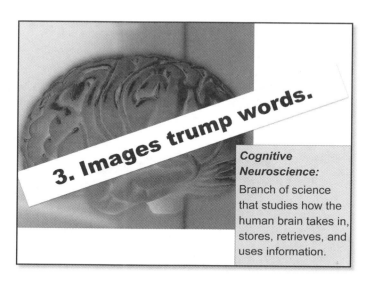

3. Images trump words.

Cognitive Neuroscience: Branch of science that studies how the human brain takes in, stores, retrieves, and uses information.

3. Images Trump Words

- *Brain Rules* author John Medina emphasizes: "Vision trumps all other senses." The brain stores images and sounds for a longer time than it does words alone. In fact, the brain seems to have an unlimited capacity for remembering mental images associated with past experiences and information learned.

- Images can come in many forms in a class or training: photos or clipart on slides and handouts, video segments, YouTube clips, verbal stories, metaphors, analogies, case studies, personal vignettes, and learner-created visuals to accompany content.

- Teachers and trainers need to include images for the major concepts being taught. Long-term memory increases when visuals accompany words.

4. Writing Trumps Reading

- *Brain Matters* author Patricia Wolfe states: "Writing and thinking are strongly linked." The brain remembers information longer when the kinesthetic act of writing is added to auditory (hearing) and visual (seeing) modalities.

- Taking notes is one way to include learner writing in a class or training. Note-taking can be done many ways: outlining, mind-mapping or concept-mapping, using both words and images (doodles or icons), using columns, drawing geometric shapes and writing in them, and using different note-taking materials.

- Teachers and trainers need to pause during content delivery and give learners opportunities to write. A minute or two of formal note-taking should be included after each important concept is covered.

5. Shorter Trumps Longer

- *Brain Rules* author John Medina explains that the brain usually "checks out" in a class at about the ten-minute mark unless something changes to catch the brain's attention again. This is due both to the brain's genetic make-up as well as cultural conditioning.

- Three examples of changes that catch the brain's attention are: media changes (using a mix of slides, charts, video clips, printed material), learner movement (engaging in short active review strategies), or demonstrations by the instructor or learners.

- Teachers and trainers need to shorten their content delivery to segments of about ten to twenty minutes. In between content segments, learners should participate in active reviews.

6. Different Trumps Same

- *Brain-Based Learning* author Eric Jensen states: "To the brain, contrast and emotion win hands down." The brain pays attention to anything that is in contrast to what came before, has sufficient emotional impact, is relevant and meaningful to the learner, or is a new (novel) learning experience. Over time, the brain begins to ignore anything that is repetitive, routine, predictable, or boring.

- Creating a learning environment that differs from traditional classes means using a variety of teaching and learning strategies instead of repeating just one or two methods of instruction or learning.

- Teachers and trainers need to engage learners in a variety of interesting and attention-catching ways.

For most readers, the top slides are the more interesting and eye-catching. While the bottom slides have more information on them, they aren't necessarily the ones that will be remembered by the brain. To find out why, turn the page and continue reading.

Images Trump Words

If I asked you to think of your office, you would probably get a mental image of the room with the furniture, computer, shelves, and materials in it. Or if I asked you to think of your family, a mental snapshot probably comes to mind. How about a procedure you or your company uses? Do you mentally see yourself doing the procedure, or do you see the print in the manual describing the procedure?

My point is that the human brain normally thinks in pictures rather than words. By pictures, I mean the mental images that the words describe. Even when learning something new and complex, humans have an easier time remembering information if there is some kind of mental image associated with it.

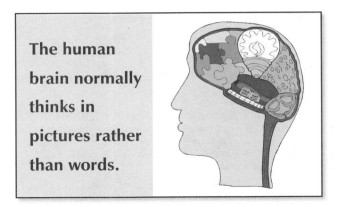

The human brain normally thinks in pictures rather than words.

Most printed materials, including the ubiquitous Powerpoint® slides found in both corporate training and educational courses, are usually devoid of images. Furthermore, most trainers and educators still use words almost exclusively when lecturing new content. Unfortunately, the words don't stick as long as we think they do.

Images stick. Images can be: stories, metaphors, analogies, vignettes, case studies, as well as cartoons, photos, graphics, maps, geometric shapes like flow charts, pie graphs, and graphic organizers (note-taking tools). Images can also be video clips or any electronic media that uses pictures.

In other words, an image is *anything* that creates a mental picture. That's why stories, metaphors, and analogies are image-rich ways to use words. Simply citing statistics or listing them on a slide is *not* an image-rich strategy. Printed material alone, whether on slides or paper, does not create a mental image unless it either describes an image or includes an actual photo or graphic that represents some part of the content.

❑❑❑❑❑❑❑

Fill-In-The-Blanks

There are four main reasons why images are so important for successful learning. Listed below are the four reasons, with the important words missing from each sentence. Use pages 129-130 to find the answers in the bold-print sentences. Then fill in the missing words in this exercise.

1. Images are a _____ _____ - _____ .

2. Images evoke _____ .

3. Images trigger _____ - _____ memory.

4. Images create _____ _____ .

Did you find all the sentences?

Put This Activity To Work: A *Fill-In-The-Blanks* activity works with slides as well as paper. Have learners guess what words are missing, or have them hunt for the missing information in the handouts, workbooks, or textbooks that you provide. Learners write the missing information and then compare their answers with yours.

If you want to do one more exercise using this principle, continue reading. If not, turn to page 72.

Adding More Images

You have a short presentation to deliver to a group of prospective students about your community college's career center. The presentation will only last about fifteen minutes. Draw a box around one or more of the options below that will have the most memorable impact on your audience.

A. You introduce yourself and show about a dozen slides as you talk about the career center's programs. On the slides are the career center's logo, bulleted lists of the certification programs, pre-certification requirements, and enrollment information. You ask if there are any questions and then thank everyone for listening.

B. You begin with your own personal career history. Then you talk about the history of the career center. You show a number of slides with career center information. You tell listeners to pick up informational brochures from the back table on the way out the door.

C. You begin with a "rags to riches" story about a student who attends a career center program and who is now a successful store manager. While you speak, listeners look at a slide photo of the happy student. You follow the story with a second slide that lists three important facts about the career center and a contact website. You pass out career center brochures that listeners can read later. You end the presentation with a quick ball toss in which listeners stand, catch the tossed ball, and state what they now know about the career center that they didn't know before your presentation.

D. You ask the listeners to tell the person seated next to them what career they think they would like to pursue while taking college classes. You refer to their chosen careers while you summarize the career center's programs, all the while showing slides of photos of students who have become certified for the jobs of their choice. The career center's website address is on each slide. You pass out flyers that have more information, and end by asking listeners to tell the person sitting next to them what their next step in choosing a career might be.

Now compare your responses to mine:

Options A and B are much less memorable because there was too much information presented in too short a time. Additionally, no images were used; the slides mainly contained words. Finally, the prospective students just sat and listened, without being actively involved at any time.

Options C and D will have a more memorable impact because they include images (slide photos and stories) and learner movement (ball-toss, pair-share). In other words, these two options are multisensory, thereby making the content easier to remember.

Did you draw boxes around Options C and D?

Even in a short fifteen-minute presentation, images can make all the difference between content that is remembered and content that is quickly forgotten.

More On Images Trump Words

When you have time, read the entire chapter in Part Three titled *Images Trump Words*. In the margins, draw logos, cartoons, or doodles of major concepts with colored markers.

Choose And Use

Below are the titles to five activities from Part Four that apply the principle *Images Trump Words*. Highlight the one that looks the most interesting to you, then turn to that page and flag it with a Post-It® note. Experiment with the activity in your next class.

1. *Say It With Symbols (page 196)*

2. *Mental Metaphors (page 199)*

3. *Story Starters (page 202)*

4. *Memory Maps (page 207)*

5. *Beat-The-Clock (page 210)*

What Have You Learned?
More Mark-Ups

Circle each sentence below that illustrates the principle *Images Trump Words*. Then compare your answers with mine.

1. Working in table groups, learners create their own conflict resolution scenarios for a management class.

2. Using a photo of the brain, train-the-trainer participants label the brain parts associated with cognitive processes.

3. An automotive instructor uses a metaphor to illustrate the difference between a two-stroke and four-stroke engine.

4. A technology trainer begins the class with a slide on which is printed the class title and learning goals listed in bulleted form.

5. Learners draw and label geometric shapes to represent steps in a data entry procedure.

6. New employees read along silently while the trainer verbally recites facts, printed on a series of slides, about the company's history.

7. In a leadership class, supervisors describe their worst-case employee/customer altercation.

8. For a computer-based training, the course content, objectives, and timelines are listed in outline format.

9. The safety manual uses illustrations to show employees how to activate a fire extinguisher.

10. Slide photos depict what prospective parents will be able to do as a result of completing a new parenting course.

11. The instructor uses a standard PowerPoint® template for all the slides he creates and all lecture content is printed on the slides.

12. Call center employees watch a short video showing acceptable phone responses to customer complaints.

13. The motorcycle safety instructor shares her own riding experiences to help new riders understand the importance of wearing safety gear.

14. Medical technicians describe how they would respond to an emergency dispatch call.

15. The slides mirror the textbook, with whole paragraphs filling the screen.

Sentences numbered 1, 2, 3, 5, 7, 9. 10, 12, 13, and 14 all illustrate the brain science principle <u>Images Trump Words</u>. While the other sentences describe common instructional situations, they do not illustrate the use of images to help learners remember content.

Put This Activity To Work: Make up your own worksheets with a list of realistic scenarios, some topic-related and some not. Tell learners to circle, underline, or check off the scenarios that illustrate topic-related concepts. Or they do the opposite: they cross out the scenarios that do not illustrate the concepts being taught.

Learning Principle Four: Writing Trumps Reading

What Would YOU Do?

Your training is about to begin and you are standing at the door, ready to hand learners two powerful learning tools as they walk in. Which two objects will you give them, or have available for them, to significantly increase their learning? Draw a star beside one answer, then turn to the indicated page.

1. A workbook and a job aid. *Turn to the top of page 76.*

2. A snack and a beverage. *Turn to the middle of page 76.*

3. A blank piece of paper and a pen/pencil. *Turn to the top of page 77.*

4. A laptop computer and manual. *Turn to the bottom of page 76.*

1. A workbook and a job aid.

   These may be necessary training materials, but they aren't the most powerful learning tools to begin a learning experience. Go back and choose another answer.

2. A snack and a beverage.

   When learners are hungry or thirsty, their capacity to learn is diminished. However, snacks and beverages aren't exactly <u>learning</u> tools. Go back and choose another answer.

4. A laptop computer and manual.

   If you chose this answer, you must have an unlimited training budget! For argument's sake, let's say you can't afford to give each learner a computer. Go back and choose another answer.

3. A blank piece of paper and a pen/pencil.

Of course! You chose this answer because you know how to transform simple writing materials into powerful learning tools.

If you want to test yourself to see how much more you already know about this learning principle, continue reading. If you want to skip ahead to an informative section, turn to *The Power of Paper* on page 79.

Circle TWO phrases that complete the following italicized sentence. Then compare your responses with mine.

Note-taking materials, such as blank paper and pens/pencils, are powerful learning tools because:

A. Learners can write notes to each other so they don't become bored.

B. Learners can use them in a variety of ways to maintain interest, engagement, and energy.

C. Learning becomes more difficult, as learners have to listen and write at the same time.

D. Learning becomes multi-sensory, meaning that the learner's body and mind are engaged when using writing materials.

For responses A and C:

A. Learners can write notes to each other so they don't become bored.

Ah, you're just kidding. You don't <u>really</u> think this is why writing materials are important learning tools, do you?

C. Learning becomes more difficult, as learners have to listen and write at the same time.

For some learners, this may be true. For most learners, writing reinforces what they've heard. Furthermore, when writing materials are used <u>correctly</u>, that is, if the instructor periodically stops talking and gives learners the opportunity to write major ideas, summaries, opinions, or questions, learning becomes easier, not to mention more interesting.

For responses B and D:

B. Learners can use them in a variety of ways to maintain interest, engagement, and energy.

You are correct. Writing materials enhance learning because they help learners review content, which reinforces it.

D. Learning becomes multi-sensory, meaning that the learner's body and mind are engaged when using writing materials.

Yes, using two or more physical senses (in this case, hearing, touch, and movement) creates a more powerful learning experience.

The Power Of Paper

Let's do a quick recap. Note-taking materials are powerful learning tools because:

▶ Learners can use them in a variety of ways to maintain interest, engagement, and energy.

▶ Learning becomes multi-sensory, which increases the brain's ability to remember data.

▶ They engage the learner's body and mind.

Writing is a kinesthetic activity because it requires physical movement (moving pen across paper). It is also tactile, which means the sense of touch is activated. Whenever more than one physical sense is used, the odds increase that learners will remember the information longer than if they just listen to it.

While learners are writing, they *can't* be thinking of anything else other than what they're writing. So their minds are totally focused on the content, which isn't the case with listening. Oftentimes, learners can fool themselves into thinking that they are listening while, in fact, they have tuned out and are thinking of other things. Not so with writing.

Just make sure you give learners time to write on the blank paper, and time to share some of what they've written. You might even stop lecturing and say, "This is profound, so write it down!"

By the way, you can use *anything* as blank paper: index cards, paper placemats, paper lunch bags, blank colored card stock, paper scraps,

Post-It® notes, sticky name tags, etc. Add colors to the mix such as multi-colored paper and multi-colored pens, pencils, or markers, and you have created some attention-catching note-taking tools.

□ □ □ □ □ □ □

Building In Writing Time

You are creating a set of PowerPoint® slides and a handout for your training. *In terms of learning,* what is the best choice to make? Draw a box around one answer below, then check your answer against mine by turning to the indicated page.

1. I will make sure all the important content is printed on the slides and in the handout. *Turn to the bottom of page 81.*

2. I will put all the important content on the slides and print them using the Powerpoint® handout format: three slides on the left side of the paper with lines for note-taking on the right side. *Turn to the middle of page 81.*

3. I will put the important content in various places in the room— slides, walls, tables—and have the learners copy much of it onto interesting note-taking pages in the handout. *Turn to the top of page 81.*

3. I will put the important content in various places in the room—
    slides, walls, tables—and have the learners copy much of it onto
    interesting note-taking pages in the handout.

    *Yes. You know that learners will remember what <u>they</u> write more
    than what <u>you</u> write. Turn the page and continue reading.*

2. I will put all the important content on the slides and print them
    using the Powerpoint® handout format: three slides on the left
    side of the paper with lines for note-taking on the right side.

    *Unfortunately, this PowerPoint® template has been vastly
    overused to the point that it is visually boring. Furthermore,
    learners might ask why they have to attend the training if all the
    content is in the handout., They could just take the handout home
    and read it later. Read answer #3 at the top of this page.*

1. I will make sure all the important content is printed on the slides
    and in the handout.

    See my response to Answer #2, in the middle of this page.

Writing Trumps Reading

As I stated in *The Power of Paper* section, learners need to have many opportunities to reflect and write during a learning experience. Because writing involves more physical senses than reading or sitting and listening without taking notes, the ability to understand and remember the content increases as well.

You have been immersed in this principle as you work through this *Choose Your Own Learning* part. The written exercises that you've completed will help you remember the concepts.

Here's a partial list of some of the written exercises you've done:

▶ *What Do You Already Know? Quick Write #1 (page 35)*

▶ *What Do You Want to Learn? Quick Write #2 (page 36)*

▶ *Summary Statement. Quick Write #3 (page 42)*

▶ *What Have You Learned? Three Card Draw (page 57)*

▶ *Fill-in-the-Blanks (page 69)*

Put This Activity To Work: Decide which of the activities listed above you plan to use in your next training. Insert one or more of the exercises into your content delivery. Use these activities to begin and end your training, as well.

The next *Data Hunt* exercise rounds out your knowledge about *Writing Trumps Reading*. If you wish to skip this exercise for now, turn to page 84.

Data Hunt

When it comes to *learning*, there are four main reasons why writing trumps reading. They are listed on page 134. Turn to those pages now, find the four bold-print sentences in the chapter, and write them on the lines below.

1. _____

2. _____

3. _____

4. _____

Read the list aloud to yourself. Then highlight the two sentences that would be the easiest for you to remember and explain to a colleague.

You just worked with this information in six ways because you:

► *Found* the concepts.

► *Read* the concepts.

► *Wrote* the concepts.

► *Reread* the concepts aloud.

► *Evaluated* the concepts in terms of your own understanding and ability to explain them to others.

► *Marked* some of the concepts by highlighting them.

Put This Activity To Work: Whenever printed data is important for the learners to read, find ways for them to interact with it. They don't need to do the same kind of interaction each time; it's the variety of activities and intermittent review of the material that will make the content easier to understand and remember.

More On Writing Trumps Reading

When you have time, read the entire chapter in Part Three titled *Writing Trumps Reading*. Create your own *Mark-Ups* with the important concepts and write your own notes in the margins.

Choose And Use

Below are the titles to five activities from Part Four that apply the principle *Writing Trumps Reading*. Highlight the one that looks the most interesting to you, then turn to that page and flag it with a Post-It® note. Use it the next time you instruct others.

1. *Mark-Ups (page 217)*

2. *Quick-Writes (page 221)*

3. *Three-Card-Draw (page 224)*

4. *Fill-In-The-Blanks (page 228)*

5. *Beat-The-Clock (page 232)*

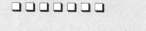

What Have You Learned?
Cross It Out

In each sentence below, cross out the phrase(s) in parentheses that is/are *not* correct. Then compare your answers with mine.

1. A main reason for using note-taking tools is to *(keep learners busy; enhance both learning and memory)*.

2. Note-taking tools are always *(things learners can write with/on; the size of a standard page of printer paper)*.

3. Note-taking is multi-sensory, meaning that *(it makes a lot of sense to use this learning strategy; it involves more than one of the physical senses: auditory, visual, kinesthetic, and tactile)*.

4. Three-Card-Draw is an example of a brain-based activity because it: *(adds novelty; increases memory through visual-spatial cues; decreases oxygen to the brain; alerts the brain to pay attention, lessens interest in the content)*.

If you crossed out the incorrect phrases, the sentences should read:

1. *A main reason for using note-taking tools is to enhance both learning and memory.*

2. *Note-taking tools are always things learners can write with/on.*

3. *Note-taking is multi-sensory, meaning that it involves more than one of the physical senses: auditory, tactile, and kinesthetic.*

4. *Three-Card-Draw is an example of a brain-based activity because it: adds novelty; increases memory through visual-spatial cues; alerts the brain to pay attention.*

Learning Principle Five: Shorter Trumps Longer

What Would YOU Do?

You have a great deal of content to cover in a short amount of time, say about three hours. You know that even if you lecture the entire time, you will be hard-pressed to cover it all. How will you divide up the three hours so that you cover the content while still engaging your learners?

The paragraphs below describe four ways you might solve this dilemma. If a paragraph portrays a traditional, teacher-centered method of instruction, label it *OLD WAY*. If it describes a brain-based, learner-centered method of instruction, label it *NEW WAY*.

A. I will divide my content into segments of about ten to twenty minutes, with quick sixty-second active review exercises between each content piece. The review activities won't take up that much time and will keep the learners engaged throughout the three hours.

B. I will basically lecture most of the content, but will include a fifteen-minute break after about ninety minutes of content delivery. I will also include a group discussion and question/answer time during the last ten minutes of class.

C. First, I will divide the content into two categories: need-to-know and nice-to-know. Then I will use a variety of instructional methods to cover the need-to-know content: short lecture segments, small group discussions, individual worksheet exercises, short flashcard games, some reading, some writing, and some learner movement. I will assign the nice-to-know content as independent reading after class.

D. I will lecture and use PowerPoint® slides and PowerPoint® handouts. I will explain to the group that I am legally obligated to cover all the content. I will encourage the learners to take notes during the lecture. Of course, I will have all the important information on the slides and handouts. Finally, I will let learners know that they can ask questions anytime they want.

Compare your answers with mine:

A. *NEW WAY.* I will divide my content into segments of about ten to twenty minutes, with quick sixty-second active review exercises between each content piece. The review activities won't take up that much time and will keep the learners engaged throughout the three hours.

"Chunking," which is dividing content into smaller segments of instruction, is a more brain-friendly way of covering a lot of material. Furthermore, inserting short, quick review activities between segments gives learners opportunities to process the new information, thereby moving the content into long-term memory.

B. *OLD WAY.* I will basically lecture most of the content, but will include a fifteen-minute break after about ninety minutes of content delivery. I will also include a group discussion and question/answer time during the last ten minutes of class.

Sometimes the old way follows the college model: fifty minutes of instruction followed by a ten-minute break. This is __not__ based on brain science. Rather, this is based on class schedules, ease of instruction, tradition, or a host of other factors that have __nothing__ to do with learning.

C. *NEW WAY.* First, I will divide the content into two categories: need-to-know and nice-to-know. Then I will use a variety of instructional methods to cover the need-to-know content: short lecture segments, small group discussions, individual worksheet exercises, short flashcard games, some reading, some writing, and some learner movement. I will assign the nice-to-know content as independent reading after class.

Often, instructors think that covering the material means that every word and every detail has to come out of the instructor's mouth. In fact, learners access information many ways. They don't have to hear it all. Furthermore, a lot of content is supplemental information, supporting the major concepts. That information can be added later, through a post-class resource or independent reading.

D. *OLD WAY.* I will lecture and use PowerPoint® slides and PowerPoint® handouts. I will explain to the group that I am legally obligated to cover all the content. I will encourage the learners to take notes during the lecture. Of course, I will have all the important information on the slides and handouts. Finally, I will let learners know that they can ask questions anytime they want.

Little, if anything, in this content-delivery scenario aids learners in remembering and using the information once the class is over.

Shorter Trumps Longer

So far, you've been exposed to short content segments sandwiched between quick activities that have engaged you even as you are learning the content. The *Choose Your Own Learning* sections have been shorter rather than longer.

In terms of learning, brain science supports this method of content delivery, *even in a book.* Sure, you can read extensive pages of content, but how much you'll remember later is open to speculation. However, when you chunk your own learning, or when it is chunked for you as it is in this book, your retention of the material will substantially increase.

Chunking means to divide content into smaller pieces or segments. We do this with lots of information: phone numbers, zip codes, letter acronyms for lengthy agency titles (think FBI, FCC), chapters in books (headings, sub-headings, paragraphs), stories (beginning, middle, end), and so on.

When chunking the content of a class, training, or workshop, a good rule of thumb is to remember the ten-minute rule. After about ten minutes of content (close enough is okay: up to twenty minutes will still work), stop talking and have your learners *do* something with the information. They can discuss the answer to a question, write a summary statement, reread their notes, stand up while discussing content, or engage in a quick, table-group summary. The point is to divide your content into short segments so that learners pay more attention to what they are hearing, understand it better, and remember it longer.

□ □ □ □ □ □ □

Chunk Your Own Learning

Here is an exercise in which you will chunk your own learning. First, look over the list below and circle one activity to do.

▸ *After reading a paragraph (or a page) of content, stop reading and write a summary statement about what you've read.*

▸ *Pretend you are explaining the paragraph (or page) to a friend: state what you just learned.*

▸ *Go back over the paragraph (or page) and highlight the main ideas or important words/phrases that you want to remember.*

▸ *Write a quiz question about the content. Come back to it later and see if you can answer it.*

▸ *Draw a star (or some kind of symbol) in the margin to mark the major idea in the paragraph or page.*

▸ *Circle or bracket the most important idea. Then, in the book's margin, write your response to this information. Examples of what you might write are: "I agree ... Want more information ... Not sure I understand ... I disagree because ..."*

Now turn to pages 136-137 and read the content. Do the activity you chose from the list above. When done, come back to this page and continue reading.

Put This Activity To Work: Provide learners with a list like the one above to choose from before they read what you've given them.

Timing The Content Segments
Quick Write #4

You will need a new index card for this *Quick Write*. On the front of the card, write some ways you could divide your content into smaller segments of instruction. For example, you might write something like the following:

▶ *I will divide the topic into subtopics, with a quick review activity between each subtopic.*

▶ *I will pause after every third slide to give learners a minute or two to discuss what they've just learned.*

▶ *I will divide my lecture material into segments of about ten or twenty minutes in length. I will rehearse delivering the content pieces while timing the rehearsal so I know how long each segment really lasts.*

On the back of the card, write your answer to the following question:

> *How will you remind yourself while you're teaching to stop and engage learners in an active review of the content?*

Some ideas to consider are: using a timer or stopwatch, posting a printed reminder, assigning a learner to give you a predetermined signal, sticking Post-It® note reminders in your lesson plans, lecture notes, or on your computer or LCD projector.

Put this index card with your lesson plan or training agenda. Then refer to it as you design/deliver the instruction.

More On Shorter Trumps Longer

When you have time, read the entire chapter in Part Four titled *Shorter Trumps Longer.* Circle, box in, or highlight the main ideas. Then write any comments or questions in the margins for later review.

Choose And Use

All of the activities in this book demonstrate the principle *Shorter Trumps Longer.* Choose one that you plan to use the next time you train, and write the title of it in the space below. If you already involve learners, write the titles of a few activities you haven't yet used.

What Have You Learned?
Check It Off

Put a check mark in front of the sentences below that illustrate the principle *Shorter Trumps Longer.*

1. The instructor's lecture lasts fifty minutes.

2. The trainer shows a series of two dozen slides as he talks.

3. The speaker stops talking after about fifteen minutes and directs learners to pair up and discuss the main ideas of the presentation.

4. The teacher announces that she will follow the forty-five minute lecture with case studies and a group game.

5. Every ten minutes, the instructor pauses to allow learners to write one-sentence summaries, engage in sixty-second paired discussions, or to stand and stretch as they think about what they've learned.

6. The trainer forgets to engage learners during an hour of training.

7. The trainer asks a learner to hold up a reminder sign so that he (the trainer) will remember to engage learners in a quick review activity every fifteen minutes.

8. The presenter tells a short story, makes a point, and then has his audience repeat a motion, phrase, or sound to drive home the point.

9. The instructor presents facts printed on slides in bullet-point format and then follows all the slides with a lengthy video illustrating the content.

10. The learners watch ten-minute video clips and, after each video, discuss the major concept illustrated by the clip.

Give yourself a pat on the back if you put a check mark in front of numbers 3, 5, 7, 8, and 10.

Learning Principle Six: Different Trumps Same

What Would YOU Do?

You are teaching a leadership class and you want to make it interesting and enjoyable for your students. Highlight the paragraph that most closely describes how you would begin the class. Then turn to the indicated page.

A. You feel it's best to begin with what students are most comfortable listening to: an introduction of yourself, an overview of the course content, expectations, timelines for assignments, when the breaks will be taken, etc. *Turn to the bottom of page 98.*

B. You feel it's best to begin with something totally unexpected like a short quiz, activity, story, or video. This is completely different from what the students have experienced in other classes. Afterwards, you will cover the more traditional opening information. *Turn to the top of page 97.*

C. You feel the best way to begin is to have each student stand and introduce himself or herself to the class, stating where they are from and why they are taking the class. *Turn to the top of page 98.*

B. You feel it's best to begin with something totally unexpected like a short quiz, activity, story, or video. This is completely different from what the students have experienced in other classes. Afterwards, you will cover the more traditional opening information.

This is an excellent way to begin the class. It is unexpected, novel, and in contrast to what students have experienced in other classes. The human brain thrives on novelty.

If you want to do another short exercise to further test what you think you already know about this principle, turn to page 99. Otherwise, turn to page 101.

C. You feel the best way to begin is to have each student stand and introduce himself or herself to the class, stating where they are from and why they are taking the class.

If you have the gift of sufficient time and the class isn't too large (less than a half-dozen), this might be acceptable. More often than not, individual introductions waste a lot of class time. Students don't remember what they've heard, they aren't connecting with each other or you, and some might be a bit embarrassed by all the attention. This type of opening is also very predictable because it is done in many classes. Now turn back to page 97 and read answer B.

A. You feel it's best to begin with what students are most comfortable listening to: an introduction of yourself, an overview of the course content, expectations, timelines for assignments, when the breaks will be taken, etc.

While keeping the students' comfort level in mind is understandable, routine and predictable openings lull students into thinking they know what is coming and therefore do not have to pay much attention. It is easy for students to tune out when a class begins like other classes. Please turn back to page 97 and read answer B.

How Different Is It?

Beside each statement below, print the letter D for *Different* if the statement describes a non-traditional or more novel way of delivering instruction and/or a more unusual way of learning. Print the letter S for *Same* if the statement describes a more traditional method of instruction and/or learning.

1. At the beginning of the class, each learner stands and introduces himself to the group.

2. As soon as learners walk into the class, they are instructed to collect topic-related facts from other learners in the room. They write these facts on index cards and will later report the facts to their table group.

3. The instructor begins the course with a humorous, topic-related anecdote.

4. The instructor begins by introducing herself and summarizing the course content.

5. As he presents, the trainer uses a set of slides with the content presented in an outline format with headers, sub-headers, and bulleted details.

6. The trainer uses a set of uncaptioned slide photos to illustrate the points she is making as she lectures.

7. During the training, learners listen and take notes on PowerPoint®-generated handouts.

8. Learners take notes on index cards, Post-It® notes, wall charts, and paper bags at different times during the training.

9. Learners stand while participating in quick, small-group discussions about the content.

10. Learners stand and toss a beach ball around the room; the thrower asks a review question and the catcher answers it.

11. The instructor asks a question and one learner raises his hand to answer. The instructor calls on him, tells him if his answer is correct, then continues the lecture.

12. The instructor asks a question and then says that the learners need to shout out at least five answers to the question.

13. The training ends with evaluations.

14. The training ends with a standing circle, in which learners take turns stating what they plan to do with what they learned.

Compare your answers with mine:

The statements that describe different ways of teaching or learning and labeled D are numbers 2, 3, 6, 8, 9, 10, 12, and 14.

The statements that describe traditional ways of teaching or learning and labeled S are numbers 1, 4, 5, 7, 11, and 13.

By the way, there is nothing wrong with the traditional activities listed above. They just don't catch the brain's attention as much as the non-traditional methods. To find out why, continue reading.

Different Trumps Same

The human brain is hardwired to notice elements in the environment that are different from what is routine or predictable. Anything that is out of the ordinary captures the brain's attention; anything routine or repetitive usually gets ignored.

The same holds true for learning environments. When these environments look like any other, the brain creates its own stimulation: it daydreams. When bored, it amuses itself. It's almost impossible for the brain to do otherwise.

Even instructional methods or learning activities that are repeated too often eventually get ignored. The implication in terms of learning is profound: *the more familiar the learning environment and instructional strategies are, the less effective they are.*

❑ ❑ ❑ ❑ ❑ ❑ ❑

Treasure Hunt

Current brain research supports the *Different Trumps Same* principle. This research can be found on page 142. Turn to these pages now and skim the information there. Then, on the treasure chest on the next page, write a few "gems" you learned from the reading.

Put This Activity To Work: The *Treasure Hunt* is a variation of the *Data Hunt* with a theme-based twist. Learners can add to their virtual treasure box of important concepts throughout the class. If you have them share their "treasures" with other learners, it serves as a quick review of what they've learned. More importantly, they will say what is important *to them* in terms of the content.

To broaden the *Treasure Hunt* activity so that it includes all six learning principles, read the *Treasure Hunt Extravaganza* on page 104.

More On Different Trumps Same

When you have time, read the entire chapter in Part Three titled *Different Trumps Same*. This time, use colored markers to color-code important concepts: red for really important, yellow for "I like this idea," green for "will use this one," and so forth. Make up your own color-coding system.

Choose And Use

Below are the titles to five activities from Part Four that apply the principle *Different Trumps Same*. Highlight the one that looks the most interesting to you, then turn to that page and flag it with a Post-It® note for later use.

1. *Dot-Voting (page 241)*

2. *Sculpt It (page 245)*

3. *Learner's Toolbox (page 249)*

4. *Looks Like, Sounds Like (page 253)*

5. *Rhythm, Rap, And Rhyme (page 256)*

Treasure Hunt Extravaganza

Let's use what is called theme-based learning and include all six principles in the next activity.

In essence, everything your classroom centers around a chosen theme. In this case, the theme is a treasure hunt. All learner activities are treasure-related, the "treasure" being the concepts you are teaching.

Picture the following descriptions in your mind, then label each description with the learning principle(s) it describes. My responses follow.

A. The slides and note-taking worksheets you create all contain various treasure-related graphics.

Learning Principle: _____

B. Before the class, you purchase small craft boxes at your local craft store. During the beginning of class, learners print their names on their "treasure boxes" and decorate them with their *Mark-Up* materials, stickers, or whatever you have on hand. During the content delivery, learners fill their boxes with concept gems: important facts, concepts, and ideas written on index cards, Post-It® notes, or small slips of paper stamped or stickered with pictures of gems.

Learning Principle: _____

C. Learners form standing pairs or triads to discuss their treasures at various times during the class.

Learning Principle: _____

D. Learners create *Treasure Hunt* presentations of content segments, with each table group presenting different concepts to the whole group as a way of reviewing what they learned.

Learning Principle: _____

E. All learning activities are short and quick, providing lots of learner involvement but without sacrificing a lot of teaching time.

Learning Principle: _____

Here are my responses:

A. *Images trump words.*
B. *Different trumps same; writing trumps reading.*
C. *Movement trumps sitting; talking trumps listening.*
D. *Movement trumps sitting; talking trumps listening; different trumps same.*
E. *Shorter trumps longer.*

Put This Activity To Work: The sky's the limit when it comes to theme-based learning. For a treasure hunt, toss in graphics of pirates, ships, flags, gems, treasure maps, costumes, prizes, and as many theme-related learning aids as you and your learners can think of. Learners get very creative when it comes to making up thematic activities.

You don't have to use the same metaphor throughout the class; you can include a few theme-related metaphors without having to go overboard (pun intended). A theme can be anything that you and your learners are interested in, or anything related to the topic.

You can find incredibly useful and detailed information about theme-based learning in author David Meier's *The Accelerated Learning Handbook* (2000, Chapter 12: *Themes*). Meier is the director of The Center for Accelerated Learning. The website at *www.alcenter.com*, is an excellent resource for brain-based learning activities.

What Have You Learned?
Three-Card-Draw Revisited

Take out your three index cards again. Look them over and add new answers to the three questions (reprinted below):

▶ **Card #1: What?** *What is one new idea you have gotten from this book so far?*

▶ **Card #2: So what?** *Why is this new idea important to you and the training work you do?*

▶ **Card #3: Now what?** *What is one way you could use this idea in your own classes?*

On a new index card, write all six learning principles:

1. *Movement trumps sitting.*

2. *Talking trumps listening.*

3. *Images trump words.*

4. *Writing trumps reading.*

5. *Shorter trumps longer.*

6. *Different trumps same.*

Tape the two cards where you will see them daily for a couple of weeks: on a bulletin board, your computer, desktop, bathroom mirror, refrigerator, dashboard, or office shelf. They are tangible reminders of what you have learned during this *Choose Your Own Learning* experience. If someone asks you about the cards, use the opportunity to explain what you wrote and why.

Bringing It Home To What You Do

The human brain is a wonderful organ.
It starts working the moment you are born
and never stops until you
stand up to teach in public.

– paraphrased from Robert Frost and George Jessel

Through this *Choose Your Own Learning* experience, you explored six learning principles that are based on twenty-first century brain science. You also participated in a variety of activities that helped you visualize how to apply the book's concepts when you instruct others. Furthermore, you discovered how to make printed material interactive.

Below is a partial list of the printed exercises you experienced. You will find most of these activities in Part Four, along with instructions for using them with the topics you teach.

▶ **Branching Stories**. You chose an answer to a question that took you to a different page or part of the printed material, depending on the answer you selected.

▶ **Data Hunt**. You read through printed text for specific information, then you marked up or recorded the information in some fashion.

▶ **Fact Or Fiction, True Or False, Old Versus New**. You labeled written statements to differentiate between opposites.

▶ **Fill-In-The-Blanks**. You filled in missing topic-related words or phrases.

▶ **Graphic Organizers**. You used note-taking materials that added a visual/spatial component to your written notes: index cards, Post-It® notes, and the book's graphics. You also drew images to represent concepts.

▶ **Mark-Ups**. You circled, highlighted, boxed, checked off, or underlined important printed content.

▶ **Quick Writes**. You thought about what you read, then wrote a sentence or summary statement about it. You also answered questions about the content, wrote what you knew before you began reading this book, and wrote your own personal learning goal.

▶ **Three-Card-Draw**. You participated in an activity that used index cards in repeated ways as graphic organizers.

▶ **Treasure Hunt**. You participated in a theme-based activity.

As you begin or expand your use of these activities, your challenge will be to remember to include them when you're in the middle of delivering content. When you're pressed for time, it's easy to fall back to the default mode of teacher-centered instruction. It's happened to all of us at one time or another.

Recognizing the difference between traditional and brain-based learning is the first step. The second step is to make a commitment to use more brain-friendly ways of instructing others. The third step is to actually change your own behavior when you teach. Finally, the fourth step is to be patient with yourself and your learners: you are changing the traditional teaching/learning paradigm, and change takes time.

What Do You Want To Learn?
Quick Write #2 Revisited

Turn back to the *Quick-Write* that you flagged on page 36. Was your personal goal met? What did you learn that was a surprise or an unexpected bonus?

Take a moment to answer the questions above on a Post-It® note or two, then put the note(s) on the graphic below.

If you still have a goal that wasn't met, or a question you would like answered, send me an email at SBowperson@gmail.com and I will do what I can to furnish the answer or supply the resources to help you find the answer yourself.

Web Warm-Ups Revisited

When you have some free time, return to page 34. Choose a website, article, YouTube video segment, or book to explore in detail. Read or watch anything related to the concepts on the *Web Warm-Ups* page that catch your interest. Make a commitment to learn more about brain science and human learning, and to share what you learn with interested colleagues, friends, and family members.

What Have You Learned?
Cross It Out

In each sentence below, cross out the phrase(s) in parentheses that is/are *not* correct. That way, the finished sentence will be correct.

1. Physical movement is crucial to effective learning because *(learning is inherently boring and movement breaks up the tedium; movement increases blood flow and oxygen to the brain, thereby enhancing cognitive function).*

2. When learners talk about what they've learned, *(they review the content again which makes it more memorable; it gives them an opportunity to chat about more interesting things, like what they will do when the class is over).*

3. The human brain *(remembers images far longer than words; remembers words far longer than images).*

4. When doing a writing exercise, learners *(can multi-task and think of other things; are totally focused on what they are writing, so retention of content is strengthened).*

5. It is easier for the human brain to remember information when content is divided into *(shorter segments of about ten to twenty minutes; longer segments of about forty to fifty minutes).*

6. The brain is hardwired to notice *(anything in the environment that changes; anything that is different from past experiences; anything that is new, or has an emotional impact; anything in the environment that is similar to other places; anything that is routine, repetitive, or predictable).*

Now compare your answers with mine. The phrases in italics below are the ones that are *not* crossed out. In other words, the entire sentence is correct.

1. Physical movement is crucial to effective learning because *movement increases blood flow and oxygen to the brain, thereby enhancing cognitive function.*

2. When learners talk about what they've learned, *they review the content again, which makes it more memorable.*

3. The human brain *remembers images far longer than words.*

4. When doing a writing exercise, learners *are totally focused on what they are writing, so retention of content is strengthened.*

5. It is easier for the human brain to remember information when content is divided into *shorter segments of about ten to twenty minutes.*

6. The brain is hardwired to notice *anything in the environment that changes; anything that is different from past experiences; anything that is new, or has an emotional impact.*

How did you do? If you missed any, write the correct sentence(s) on an index card to help reinforce the correct information.

Choose Your Own Learning:
What Was It Like For YOU?

As a concluding exercise, take a few moments to reflect on this entire *Choose Your Own Learning* experience. Write your responses to the following questions on the back of this page:

1. *How is what you now know different from what you knew before you began working through this book?*

2. *How do you plan to use what you've learned?*

3. *What has this interactive learning experience been like for you?*

4. *What do you see as the benefits and drawbacks of learning this way?*

5. *In terms of your own learning, what are the exercises that really worked well for you? Why?*

As the author, I would really appreciate knowing your answers to the above questions. Your responses will help me determine how to format the sequel to this book. I want to know which types of exercises were most beneficial, which to let go of, and the overall learning impact of the "branching story" format. Please email your responses, comments, or suggestions to SBowperson@gmail.com. I will appreciate any feedback you send.

Congratulations on completing this *Choose Your Own Learning* adventure!

A great learning journey starts in the middle!
Michael Allen

PART THREE

Six Learning Principles That Trump Traditional Teaching

The Six Trumps®

Trump *(noun)*:
A suit in card games that outranks all others;
a key resource to be used at an opportune moment.

To trump *(verb)*:
To get the better of something or someone else by using
a crucial, often hidden resource;
to excel, surpass, outdo.
– from a variety of online dictionaries

In Part One, I used the metaphor of a card game to describe ways of learning that trump other, more traditional learning methods. When one learning strategy trumps another, it means it is a more effective way to learn.

If you have read Parts One and Two of this book, you are already familiar with the six learning principles that trump more traditional ways of learning:

1. *Writing trumps reading.*

2. *Movement trumps sitting.*

3. *Talking trumps listening.*

4. *Images trump words.*

5. *Shorter trumps longer.*

6. *Different trumps same.*

I am not suggesting that we totally eliminate the ways most learners have traditionally been taught: by sitting, listening, reading, or being in long classes that use the same delivery and learning methods.

I *am* suggesting that, *in terms of learning,* traditional methods are far less effective than those that engage learners during the entire learning process through movement, discussion, imagining, and writing. There is considerable brain science to support the paradigm shift from traditional "sit down, be still, and listen" learning to more brain-based and brain-friendly learning experiences. Furthermore, the brain science indicates that these non-traditional learning methods are also more body-friendly.

The next six chapters explore the six learning principles in detail. You will also be introduced to many of the authors whose research adds to the growing body of brain science about human learning.

Brain *(noun):*
An apparatus with which we think that we think.

Ambrose Pierce

Learning Principle One:
Movement Trumps Sitting

Physical activity is cognitive candy.

John Medina

You've been sitting for a long stretch of time, perhaps at work at your computer, or perhaps in a meeting or workshop. You recognize the

physical feelings that accompany your lack of physical motion: lethargy, muscle stiffness, a general tiredness, and a decrease in your mental and physical energy.

Now remember those feelings as you think about the last time you were a learner in a traditional-style classroom setting. How well did you learn the material? How much did you remember after an hour or more of sitting?

Here is a fact so profoundly simple yet so ignored in most traditional classrooms that it should be a mandatory part of every train-the-trainer program and teacher education course:

The longer learners sit, the less they learn.

Molecular biologist John Medina has written a brilliant book titled *Brain Rules* (2008) in which he makes the case for the necessity of physical motion in the daily lives of human beings. Medina says that the human body is genetically designed to move. Our ancient survival as a species was based on movement: hunting for food, escaping from predators, and constantly adapting to changes in our physical environment.

The sedentary lifestyle many of us lead now—in offices, classrooms, cubicles, meeting rooms, and in our homes—is extremely detrimental to our physical and mental well-being. "Whether learning or working, we gradually quit exercising the way our ancestors did. The result is like a traffic wreck" (Medina, 2008, p. 23). Medina goes on to say that our sedentary life style is, in fact, causing or exacerbating many of the diseases related to mental decline.

Medina's bottom line is simple: "Exercise boosts brain power" (p. 7). He elaborates, "We can make a species-wide comeback. All we have to do is move" (pp. 22-23). We *think* better when we insert movement into our daily activities, including those places where we sit a lot.

Let's bring motion into the learning environment. Here are four specific reasons why learners need to move:

1. Movement Enhances Cognition

It's basic physiology. When learners move, blood circulation increases and more oxygen flows to the brain. Neurons (brain cells) work more effectively when they get more oxygen.

Short activities spaced throughout the class are better for brain function than sitting for an hour or more. In the classroom, activities as simple as a standing stretch or walking in place are beneficial to learning.

2. Movement Boosts Memory

Multi-sensory learning means using more than one physical sense to learn: auditory (hearing), visual (seeing), kinesthetic (moving), tactile (touching), olfactory (smelling), and gustatory (tasting). With multi-sensory learning, more neurons are stimulated which makes the learning experience more memorable.

3. Movement Keeps Learners Awake

As a trainer, you probably move around a lot when you teach so you have no problem remaining awake and alert. Your brain benefits enormously because of your movement.

Now, what about your learners? There is no rule that says they have to remain seated. Not one teaching manual or training course says that learners cannot stand up between lecture segments or even while you are talking.

Learners wake up when they stand up.

Learners wake up when they stretch. Learners wake up when they turn and talk to other learners. Learners wake up when they walk to another part of the room. Any movement, however small, will help learners stay awake and alert.

4. Movement Increases Energy

Any type of motion also increases physical energy. More oxygen equals more energy. More energy equals better learning. I'm repeating myself here because many of us (present company excepted) still forget to stop periodically in the middle of our lectures to allow learners to move, write, and talk.

The Bottom Line

Prevent death by sitting!
Get learners to <u>move</u>.

What's In It For You?

What are you taking away from this chapter that is useful *to you?* Write a short summary of the principle *Movement Trumps Sitting* on a Post-It® note. On another note, write one change that you will make in one of your classes as a result of this principle. Then place both

Post-It® notes on the image below. By doing this, you will remember and use the principle the next time you teach.

You have brains in your head,
You have feet in your shoes.
You can steer yourself
Any direction you choose.

Dr. Seuss

❑ ❑ ❑ ❑ ❑ ❑ ❑

Learning Principle Two:
Talking Trumps Listening

The best way to learn something is to teach it.
Patricia Wolfe

We are, by nature, a social species. Long ago, our ancestors learned that they had a better chance of surviving if they cooperated with each other rather than compete. Cooperation led to faster skills ac-

quisition because adults taught what they knew about survival to their young and to other adults. Through cooperation, our ancestors became more knowledgeable and more skilled while increasing their odds for survival.

Somewhere along the centuries-old path of education, the cooperation paradigm shifted to one of passive, individualized, non-interactive learning: sitting at a desk, listening to a lecture or lesson, passing a test, and doing it over and over again. This model never really worked all that well, and still doesn't. It completely undermines the power of cooperation and social engagement in learning.

Technology expert, elearning guru, and author Jay Cross, in his outstanding book *Informal Learning* (2007), explains:

> *We've outgrown the definition of learning as the activity of an individual ... we humans exist in networks. Learning consists of making and maintaining better connections to our networks.*

Cross sums it up by saying, "Learning is social. We learn from, by, and with other people" (p. 63).

Returning for a moment to our ancestors, they had to learn how to communicate in order to cooperate. From rudimentary gestures and sounds, our most common form of communication evolved: verbal language. Our ancestors learned to verbally explain, respond, argue, vent, engage, ask, answer, teach, encourage, coach, and share.

Today, we do the same. We talk so that we can understand. We talk so that we can remember.

We talk so that we can learn.

And yes, listening is a part of cooperation, communication, and learning. But, especially in formal learning environments, listening is often the only thing learners do. The truth is, listening should be the *smallest* part of the entire learning process. To learn best, learners listen and watch, write and talk, demonstrate and practice, then *teach what they've learned to someone else.* It is in the talking about it and teaching it that learners begin to master the material.

Here are five specific reasons why learner discussions are powerful ways to strengthen learning:

1. Talking Increases Retention
When learners verbally explain something they have just learned, they process the information three times: first, they hear it; second, they think about it; third, they restate it in their own words. It's as if they have stepped into the role of the teacher. When they teach, they increase the probability of understanding and internalizing the information better. Even a simple, one-minute paired discussion about what they heard will help learners remember more than if they didn't discuss the material.

2. Talking Builds Relationships
Medina reminds us: "Our ability to learn has deep roots in relationships" (2008, p. 45).

> *If someone does not feel safe with a teacher or boss [or other learners], he or she may not be able to perform as well ... relationships matter when attempting to teach human beings (p. 46).*

When learners talk to each other, they form relationships for at least the duration of the learning experience. These relationships are just as important to the success of the learning as the content. Why? Because relationships create a feeling of psychological safety. When learners feel safe with each other and the instructor, they are more willing to ask questions, make mistakes, be open to new ideas, try new skills, and take some risks. In effect, they learn better.

3. Talking Creates Meta-Learning

Meta-learning means learning about learning. This is what happens when learners have the time to discuss not only the content, but also how they learned it, their understanding of it, and how it links to what they already know.

Meta-learning also means that learners take charge of their own learning: asking questions, soliciting feedback, offering opinions, and changing what isn't working for them. When they do this, they feel empowered. "Setting people up to learn how to learn ignites a process of perpetual self-improvement. Enlightened self-interest kicks in" (Cross, 2007, p. 78).

4. Talking Elicits Feedback

During the natural give-and-take of a conversation, learners have opportunities to give and receive feedback about their understanding of the content. They can correct each other's misperceptions or offer alternative ways of looking at the same material. By doing so, they deepen their own under-

standing of the material. Moreover, you don't have to re-teach as much when learners can discuss the content and ask questions amongst themselves.

5. Talking Enhances Self-Worth

Everyone likes to be listened to. Everyone likes to share what he or she knows: facts, opinions, theories, and prior knowledge about the topic. When learners have opportunities to talk to each other, their sense of self-worth increases. Who they are and what they know matters to the group. The learners benefit, the group benefits and, ultimately, the whole learning experience is strengthened.

The Bottom Line

*The person doing the most talking about the topic
is doing the most learning about the topic.*

What's In It For You?

Think about what you now know about the principle *Talking Trumps Listening*. On the notepad below, write a short summary of what you've learned and how you will use this information the next time you instruct others.

A brain is worth little without a tongue.
French Proverb

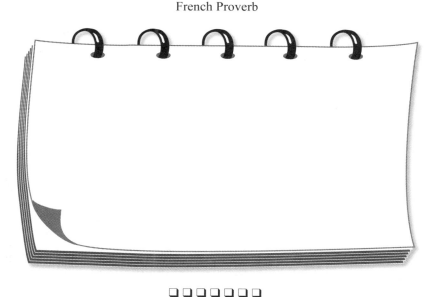

Learning Principle Three: Images Trump Words

*We do not see with our eyes;
we see with our brains.*

John Medina

Pay attention to what goes on in your mind as you read each of the following two-word phrases:

Mickey Mouse
ocean waves
best friend
night sky
first love
ice cream

Did you get a mental image of the person, place, or thing the words described? Or did you simply see the printed words spelled out in your mind's eye?

The probability is quite high that your brain created images instead of just seeing the words printed on this page. In fact, whenever a printed concept (in this case, a specific person, place, or thing) describes an image, you will usually recall the image first. Furthermore, according to Medina, "The more visual the input becomes, the more likely it is to be recognized—and recalled" (2008, p. 233).

We remember images. We forget words.

If we *do* remember words alone, they usually describe images or are combined with images to make the words more memorable. Think: stories, metaphors, and analogies. If we combine the words with rhythm, rhyme, and repetition, the words quickly move into long-term memory. Think: songs, poems, rap, commercials, and slogans. And if we combine the words with moving images such as videos, the content becomes almost unforgettable.

Patricia Wolfe, an expert on the educational implications of brain science and author of the book *Brain Matters* (2001), states, "The capacity for long-term memory of pictures seems almost unlimited" (p. 153). According to Wolfe, most, if not all, of our memories are stored as images and sounds, not words. We then use words to describe what we are seeing and hearing inside our heads.

Cross elaborates:

> *We humans are sight mammals. We learn almost twice as well from images plus words as from words alone. Pictures translate across cultures, education levels, and age groups ... because the richness of the whole picture can be taken in at a glance* (2007, p. 117).

Given the power of images to teach, why are many classrooms so lacking in images? Why do many teachers persist in presenting information without stories, metaphors, analogies, photographs, graphics, or videos? Why is PowerPoint® still primarily used as a text-only medium? Pause here and think about *your* answers to these questions, then read my opinion below.

Three reasons come to my mind: habit, modeling, and time. We are used to presenting information primarily as a collection of facts. We have gotten in the habit of doing this after we were taught to teach that way: linearly, logically, fact-by-fact. We've seen instruction modeled that way over and over again. And, once we learned the fact-based, lecture-based model, we realized that it's a time-efficient way of delivering a lot of information. Notice that I did not say it is an effective way to *learn*.

Let's get specific. Do you put your lecture notes on slides and read from them? While this may help *you* with content delivery, it doesn't enhance *learning*. It doesn't make the content easier to remember. In fact, the opposite usually happens: learners tune out. They can't help it. The brain is searching the environment (both internal and external) for more interesting things to focus on.

When you add relevant images, even simple ones, to your lecture material, the entire learning experience changes for the better. Medina explains:

> *There are things we know about how pictures grab attention that are rock solid. We pay lots of attention to color. We pay lots of attention to size. And we pay special attention if the object is in motion* (2008, p. 237).

Here are four specific reasons why you should include images when you train:

1. Images Are A Brain Turn-On

Let's face it, the human brain *loves* images. The more sensory the image is—detailed, colorful, eye-catching, descriptive, emotional—the longer the brain stays interested in it. Stories are a great example of this. Whether strictly verbal (hearing a story) or both verbal and pictorial, such as the Internet, television and movies, learners will pay more attention and stay focused longer whenever images are used to teach content.

2. Images Evoke Emotions

It is almost impossible for the human brain to remain focused on anything that is totally devoid of emotion. Why? Because emotion is the brain's signal to pay attention. Educator and author Robert Sylwester, in his brain-science book *A Celebration of Neurons* (1995), makes the short but profound observation: "Emotion drives attention, which drives learning and memory" (p. 86). So, without emotion, neither learning nor memory function well.

Images evoke emotional reactions in learners when sometimes words alone can't. The images can be humorous or serious, simple (graphics) or complex (videos). The emotional impact will exist regardless of the medium. When learners react emotionally to images, they pay attention longer and remember more about the content later.

3. Images Trigger Long-Term Memory

As I pointed out in the last section, long-term memory relies on images and the emotions that go with them. The more image-rich and emotionally evocative you can make your content, the more it will stick.

There is no such thing as non-emotional long-term memory. Anything that is totally devoid of emotion will most likely be forgotten in a short amount of time unless a special effort is made by the learners to remember. According to Wolfe, "The brain is biologically programmed to attend first to information that has strong emotional content" (2001, p. 87).

4. Images Create Short-Cuts

It takes time to describe even a simple procedure. Think of telling someone how to brush his teeth, for example. It takes far less time to demonstrate tooth-brushing, or to watch a video of people brushing their teeth. From a learning perspective, the verbal description of tooth-brushing means that the learner has to translate the words into mental images. When the learner watches the demonstration or video, no translation from words to picture is necessary.

Images can greatly shorten the amount of teaching time needed for effective learning transfer. Images help learners translate information into action, without having to put everything into words first.

The Bottom Line

> *When they picture it,*
> *and feel it,*
> *they get it.*

What's In It For You?

Inside the picture frame below, create two simple images (think of them as doodles). The first represents the most important concept you've learned about the principle *Images Trump Words*. The second represents how you plan to use this information the next time you teach.

> *My girlfriend and I went on a picnic.*
> *I don't know how she did it,*
> *but she got poison ivy on the brain.*
> *When it itched,*
> *the only way she could scratch it*
> *was to think about sandpaper.*
>
> Steven Wright

Learning Principle Four: Writing Trumps Reading

Notes are an active learning tool ...
Revisit to remember.

Jay Cross

How do you help yourself remember a friend's new address or phone number? You probably write it down or enter the information into an electronic device and/or cell phone. What about remembering an appointment? You make a note on your calendar. Important information you've discussed with colleagues at a lunch meeting? Napkin-writing is pretty common. How about the things you need to pick up at the store? A shopping list does the trick.

We write to remember.
We remember because we write.

The two go hand-in-hand. The *act* of writing plays an important part in remembering *what* we write.

When learners take notes, they are using a powerful learning tool. The notes will not only help them recall important information later, but will also help them understand the information better than if they just listened and did nothing else.

In traditional training programs and educational classes, who is usually doing the most writing? More often than not it's the instructor. Who writes on the chart paper? The trainer. Who writes on the chalkboard or white board? The teacher. Who creates the slides and handout materials? The instructor. What are learners doing while all this is going on? Usually sitting, passively watching and listening (or not—it's impossible to tell if learners are listening or daydreaming).

I have to acknowledge here that I've been admonished by a college teacher who says that her students always take notes. Perhaps that is your experience with your learners, as well. The next time you attend a class as a learner, though, I challenge you to observe who does most of the writing: the instructor or the other learners. The answer might surprise you.

The instructor may even suggest that learners take notes. But the percentage of learners who actually do this is small. Why? Because most learners have been *conditioned* to sit and listen without doing anything else. Additionally, if truth be told, most learners don't know *how* to take notes, that is, to identify major ideas and to be able to separate the need-to-know from the nice-to-know information.

Cross says that most people "haven't thought about learning to learn. It's not what they have been conditioned to do in the workplace, and it's rarely taught" (2007, p. 79). If learners haven't been taught as children to write down key words and phrases as they listen, then they probably won't think to do that as adults.

So why take notes? Cross explains: "Taking notes is a valuable form of processing information … known to increase the likelihood of understanding and remembering material" (p. 78). He continues: "Learning requires time to sink in. Don't let scrambling to meet the clock crowd out time for reflection" (p. 11). Wolfe adds: "Writing and thinking are strongly linked. Writing serves as a tool for refining thinking" (2001, p. 171).

When learners write (or draw symbols for) key words, phrases, or concepts, they process the spoken information three times: once in hearing it; the second time in thinking about it; and the third time in translating it into a written form.

With that said, here are four specific reasons why writing is a powerful learning tool:

1. Writing Stimulates Memory

Learners remember what *they* write, not necessarily what *you* write. Writing activates parts of the brain that aren't used when learners simply listen or read. When learners write, their brain stores the information differently so that it is more accessible later.

2. Writing Is Kinesthetic

Learners remember *because* they write. It is the physical act of moving a pen across a page that makes writing a better learning strategy than listening alone. The movement stimulates the brain and the senses. The conversation between the brain and the hand helps cement the learning.

3. Writing Is Visual-Spatial

Learners remember *where* they write. They get a mental picture of the *location* of specific bits of information on a piece of paper: top, bottom, side, middle. The addition of visual cues such as color, graphics, geometric shapes, fill-in-the-blanks, connecting lines, and the like will create mental images of the content, making it even more memorable. But *learners* have to do the writing, not you.

4. Writing Grabs Attention

It's almost impossible for learners to write one thing while thinking another. When the human brain is involved in writing, it *has* to think about the writing, at least until the writing is finished. That is *not* the case with listening. Most lecture-based instruction conditions learners to listen with only part of the brain engaged; the other part is daydreaming or thinking about other things. I'm sure you've experienced this yourself: drifting in and out of conscious attention. However, when learners write about what they have just heard, they are totally focused on content.

The Bottom Line

Learners remember what <u>they</u> write
better than what <u>you</u> write.

What's In It For You?

On a Post-It® note, write a one or two-sentence summary of the principle *Writing Trumps Reading*. Add a symbol that respresents what you wrote and put the note on the image below.

Have you tried neuroxing papers?
It's a very easy and cheap process.
You hold the page in front of your eyes
and you let it go through there into the brain.
It's much better than xeroxing.

Sydney Brenner

Learning Principle Five: Shorter Trumps Longer

Space out the input.
John Medina

Television stations know it. Advertisers know it. Children know it. Even most adults know it, albeit subconsciously. What it is that we all know? Simply put, the human brain likes learning small "chunks" of information that are followed by short breaks of some kind.

I've pointed out in many of my previous books that, in a television-saturated country such as the United States, where the average amount of television watched in a day is four hours, generations of learners have been conditioned to receive their information in short segments. From Sesame Street for children to news broadcasts for adults, we get our information doled out in chunks of about ten minutes with commercial breaks in between. And what do we do during the commercial breaks? Talk, wriggle, stand up, walk, and otherwise move in various ways.

This chunking is not accidental. Television producers and advertisers know a thing or two about the human brain. For example, they know about how long the brain will focus before losing interest. They know the power of images in holding attention. And they know movement stimulates neurons, whether the movement is on the screen or between content segments.

In other words, television is, in many ways, a very brain-compatible learning medium. It is image-rich with highly contrasting visuals, lots of movement and change, and full of new information and situations which stimulate the brain. The variety can hold the viewer's attention for hours. Furthermore, as in the case with full-length movies, television stimulates emotions which put the images into long-term memory.

Of course, there are many arguments to be made for television's negative impact on the human attention span, that is, the ability to concentrate on one thing without becoming distracted. But, for those of us who teach for a living, there are lessons to be learned in terms of delivering content.

I am not suggesting that we change the complexity of the content we teach, or that we dumb it down. I *am* suggesting that we chunk the content into short segments followed by quick "commercials"— short, interactive topic-related reviews that get learners moving while discussing the content just covered.

Medina has gathered a lot of evidence in the college courses he teaches that support the ten-minute rule, meaning that students' minds begin to drift after about ten minutes of traditional lecture. According to Medina, something has to change every ten minutes in order to hold students' attention. His research supports what television producers and advertisers have known for years. He explains:

> *Before the first quarter-hour is over in a typical presentation, people usually have checked out. What happens at the ten-minute mark to cause such trouble? ... The brain seems to be making choices according to some stubborn timing pattern, undoubtedly influenced by both culture and gene* (2008, p. 74).

One solution to this attention issue is "to incorporate new information gradually and repeat it in timed intervals" (Medina, 2008, p. 147). In other words, present a short content segment and then follow it with a short movement/review break. After that, cover another content segment and follow it with another active review break.

Remember the ten-minute rule: content segments should be about ten minutes in length and no more than twenty. Active review breaks can be a minute or two—just long enough for learners to take a break from passive listening. Have them talk about what they've heard, write down key points, state an opinion about it, ask or answer a question about it. If they've learned a physical skill, have them actually demonstrate it.

Here are four specific benefits to dividing your content into segments of about ten to twenty minutes:

1. Learners Remain Alert
As I've mentioned, learners find it easier to stay awake and alert when there are short segments of instruction followed by one or two minutes of active review. The brain doesn't have time to wander off the topic and think of other things. The quick review activities enhance oxygen flow to the brain, especially if the review includes movement.

2. Learners Stay Engaged
When a quick review activity follows each lecture segment, learners become accountable for remembering the content. So they listen more carefully and pay more attention to what they are hearing.

3. Learning Becomes Collaborative
When learners are accountable for remembering the content, they learn from and teach each other as they review important concepts. Thus, they work together and support each other in the learning. The entire learning experience changes from an individual one to a collaborative one.

4. You Polish Your Content
A sculptor cuts away extraneous stone and polishes the piece of art she has created. So, too, dividing information into smaller content segments means that you have to get clear about what the core, need-to-know concepts are. Also, with shorter segments of instructional time, you realize you have to let go of nice-to-know details that might

not be important to the overall learning. It will take more behind-the-scenes planning time to do this. However, the payoff will come during the direct instruction because your content will be short, concise, and to-the-point.

The Bottom Line

The longer you talk, the less they learn.

What's In It For You?

What are some specific ways you might apply the principle *Shorter Trumps Longer?* In the picture frame below, draw a few doodles that summarize what you've learned and how you will use it in when training.

The brain is designed to grab what input it can and then to boil it up into a froth of understanding.

John McCrone

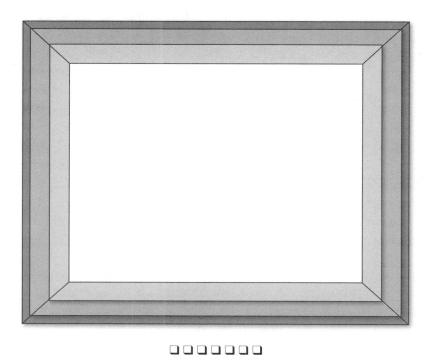

❑ ❑ ❑ ❑ ❑ ❑ ❑

Learning Principle Six:
Different Trumps Same

*To the brain, contrast and emotion
win hands-down.*

Eric Jensen

When you think about it, it makes perfect sense: we notice things in our environment that have changed and ignore things that remain the same. Our ancestors depended upon this ability for their survival. They *had* to pay attention to the changes in the environment to determine if danger lurked. For example, bushes rustling a hundred feet away might have meant a predator was stalking them. Storm clouds and sudden winds meant they should take shelter quickly. When the environment presented no changes, our ancestors could relax and focus on tasks like preparing a meal or watching their young. They didn't need to spend time or energy paying attention to the environmental elements when these elements remained the same.

In his book *Brain-Based Learning* (2000), author and member of the International Society for Neuroscience, Eric Jensen, explains: "Any stimuli introduced into our immediate environment, which is either new (novel) or of sufficiently strong emotional intensity (high contrast), will immediately gain our attention" (p. 122).

The human brain works the same way in learning environments. We notice things that are different from before, that evoke an emotional response, or are meaningful to us in some way. We quickly tune out the things that don't change or that don't interest us, thereby freeing up our minds for more interesting thoughts. In fact, we pay little conscious attention to anything that we determine is routine, repetitive, predictable, or just downright boring.

When covering dry or very technical material, some instructors say to their learners, "This is boring but we have to cover it." *Boring is brain-antagonistic.* Boring means little or no learning takes place. As you've just learned, the brain is hard-wired to screen out boring stuff. The longer the content remains boring, the harder it is for learners to pay attention. And, while the information may be dry, technical, or complex, *the delivery of it doesn't have to be boring.*

You might be thinking, "But too much stimulation, too much change in the learning environment, can make people anxious, uneasy, or stressed." Yes, you're right. It's a balancing act between making things different and keeping things the same. Too much of the former stresses the brain; too much of the latter bores the brain.

The trick is to change little things while maintaining an overall consistency in the big things. For example, you probably have a certain order in which informational pieces must be presented so that the content builds on itself. Within this order—this *flow* of information—you can change lots of little things: where you stand, your movements, gestures, voice tone, speaking pace, and so on.

You can also change your learners' participation by using paired discussions, quick written summaries, short question/answer segments, table discussions, worksheet fill-ins, and the like. Small changes to your delivery methods and increased learner engagement will help keep learner attention and interest high.

Here are four specific reasons why you need to use a variety of instructional methods and learning activities:

1. The Brain Responds To Novelty

Again, anything new in the learning environment, including your delivery, will catch learners' attention. Newness is addictive to the human brain. Of course, the new activities will become repetitive and routine if used too long or too often. Variety is important to maintain learner attention and motivation.

2. The Brain Responds To Contrast

As Jensen points out, anything that is different from what came before also wakes up the brain. The higher the contrast, the more attention grows. In a learning environment, contrast can be physical: learners move from place to place in the room. It can be visual: learners look at photos on slides or watch a video. It can be emotional: you recount a touching or exciting story or learners share their own topic-related stories. Or it can be a mixture of all of the above.

3. The Brain Responds To Emotion

I know this sounds like a broken record but, even with what brain scientists tell us about the power of emotion, in traditional classrooms emotion is still undervalued and seldom consciously used during content delivery.

Often instructors simply say, "This is important, so pay attention." There is little positive emotional context in that. Consequently, learners forget most of the content quite rapidly. On the other hand, when instructors are passionate about their topics, and the learning experience is an exciting and positive one, learners become emotionally involved in the experience which, in turn, increases long-term retention.

4. The Brain Responds To Meaning

In order for the learning to stick, it must be meaningful *to the learner*. Somehow, the content must connect to something the learner feels is important, to what the learner already knows, or to the learner's personal life and work. This is true regardless of the age or experience of the learner. A child still needs to know that what he is learning *has meaning for him*. So does an adult.

It is your responsibility to help your learners find meaning and relevancy. Saying, "You need to learn this now because you'll need it later on" doesn't cut it. Saying, "Here's how you can use this today" does.

The Bottom Line

> *Novelty, meaning, emotion, contrast:*
> *These are the keys to make learning last.*

What's In It For You?

How do you plan to use the principle *Different Trumps Same* in your own instruction? Summarize the chapter on Post-It® notes, then write your action plan. Put your notes on the image below.

> *I wish my name was Brian*
> *because maybe sometimes people would*
> *misspell my name and call me Brain.*
> *That's like a free compliment and you don't*
> *even gotta be smart to notice it.*
>
> Mitch Hedberg

Counting Your Cards

Sometimes the best thing to do
is to shuffle the cards again.
Camilo Jose Cela

In a card game, you usually count your cards or the total points scored at the end of the game. Let's count (review) the learning principles one more time. On the next page, see if you can list the six principles from memory, in any order. When you're done, go back through the chapters to check if you got them all.

Of course, the challenge will be for you to apply them whenever you teach. Post the principles as reminders on the walls of the classroom. Explain them to the learners. Label your content segments and review exercises with the principles they demonstrate. Use colored markers and assign a specific color to each principle. Then color-code your lesson plans. Make yourself a promise to use at least one principle in each class you conduct.

Sooner than you think, these principles will become second nature to you. Eventually, you will be the one who teaches this brain science to others. You will become, to quote a friend of mine, the "Six Trumps Expert!"

Someday the cellophane
will crackle off a fresh deck of cards,
one that belongs to you,
and the cards will be stacked in your favor.
Pat Riley

Learning Principle: _____

_____

Learning Principle: _____

_____

Learning Principle: _____

_____

Learning Principle: _____

_____

Learning Principle: _____

_____

Learning Principle: _____

_____

What Did You Get From This Book?
Benefits Revisited

The principal activity of the brain
is making changes in itself.
Marvin Minsky

On page 27 you highlighted the benefits from this book that were the most important *to you*. Go back to those pages now and reread the benefits that you highlighted.

Take a moment to reflect on what you have learned from this book and how it might change your classroom instruction. If you teach online or design computer-based courses, how will you apply the principles to your courses? Write your thoughts in the margins on this page.

What surprises did you get or unexpected benefits did you receive while reading this book? Write your answers in the margins.

What topics would you like to know more about? Send a reminder email to yourself or leave a message for yourself on your work phone to do an Internet search for these topics.

Finally, what concepts do you think are important enough, and useful enough, to share with colleagues? Write your answers in large print on a piece of paper and post it where others can see it. When they ask you about it, explain the concepts to them.

My book editor and friend, Phyllis Van, says that this is the most important trump of all:

Teaching trumps everything!

In other words:

> *You master <u>what</u> you teach*
> *<u>when</u> you teach it.*

So spread the word. Let others know what you've learned. Show them or tell them what you are doing with the concepts from this book, and congratulate yourself for knowing what you know.

> *It is not unreasonable to expect that*
> *the brain will continue to study itself*
> *so long as Homo Sapiens last.*
> Pinckney Harmon

PART FOUR

Putting The Principles To Work

Getting Started

To begin with, you must realize
that any idea accepted by the brain
is automatically transformed
into an action of some sort.
It may take seconds or minutes or longer,
but ideas always lead to action.

Scott Reed

Putting the learning principles to work is easier than you think. If you already engage learners as you teach, then simply add to what is working well. If you aren't quite sure how to involve learners yet, the strategies and activities in this part of the book will get you there.

Of course, whether you are experienced or not, your challenge will be to remember to apply the learning principles while decreasing the time you spend using traditional methods of instruction. This is a process, not an end result.

In this part of the book, I use the word "strategy" to mean a general approach to applying the principle. A strategy is something *you* do. *Keep it short* is a strategy. I use the word "activity" to describe a specific interactive technique and something the *learner* does. A *Body Break* is an activity.

All the strategies and activities are simple to use. You can easily change most of them to fit your topics and audiences. Some are variations from my previous books; others are new ones I've created or collected along the way.

Listed below are ten general strategies that apply to all the learning principles:

▶ **Let Go Of Comfort**. Challenge yourself to step out of *your* comfort zone. Experiment with non-traditional instructional methods and learner involvement. The positive responses you receive from learners will reinforce the changes you make.

▶ **Time For Confidence**. Give yourself time to get used to these new methods. Yes, stepping out of your comfort zone is important, but it's equally important to gain a level of confidence that comes from feeling comfortable with the activities.

▶ **Engagement, Not Perfection**. Aim for learner engagement, not activity perfection. If an activity does not go exactly as planned, it can still be a powerful learning experience.

▶ **Combine Them**. Often, one activity actually includes more than one learning principle. For example, a one-minute standing *Turn And Talk* applies *Movement Trumps Sitting, Talking Trumps Listening, Shorter Trumps Longer,* and *Different Trumps Same.*

▶ **Use The Ten-Minute Rule**. Divide your content into segments of about ten minutes in length (a guideline, not an absolute). In between each content segment, insert a short review activity that applies one or more of the learning principles.

▶ **Keep It Short**. Most of the exercises take no more than a few minutes. Many take a minute or less. They are easy to insert into traditional instruction without losing much lecture time. If you alternate between short instructional segments and short review activities, the significant increase in learning and retention will surprise you.

▶ **Mix Them Up**. Use a variety of both instructional strategies and learning activities. When you do choose to repeat a certain activity (a *Body Break*, for example), vary it just a bit to make it different from the previous *Body Break*.

▶ **Group Management Signal**. Before engaging learners in any activity, be sure to explain and demonstrate a group management signal. The signal can be auditory such as a whistle, bell, musical piece, a rhythmic clap, or a verbal cue. It can be visual such as a sign you hold up, flicking the room lights off and on, or a raised hand. Or the signal can be a combination of both auditory and visual cues. The signal will do two things: show that the activity has ended and tell learners to turn their attention back to you.

▶ **The Right To Pass**. This is a psychological safety net that learners need in order to step out of *their* comfort zone and learn in new ways. You explain that, whenever an activity occurs, learners have the right to pass: they can choose to observe rather than participate. Most won't ever need to use this safety net; a few might. Once these few feel psychologically comfortable, they will join the group of active learners.

▶ **Use What Works**. Use an activity a few times before evaluating its effectiveness. Then decide whether or not to keep it, let it go, or try something else. What works for one group of learners may not work as well for another. Enlist the aid of the learners themselves to make the activities work better.

The Bottom Line. Trust your judgment. Go with your gut. Let the learners shine!

You shake my nerves and you rattle my brain.
Jerry Lee Lewis

The Six Trumps® Revisited

In terms of learning:

1. ***Movement trumps sitting.*** Motion increases oxygen to the brain, which also increases cognitive function.

2. ***Talking trumps listening.*** Learners understand and remember more whenever they engage in short discussions about the content.

3. ***Images trump words.*** For long-term retention, visual input is far more powerful than auditory input alone.

4. ***Writing trumps reading.*** Learners remember content longer when they write it rather than just read it.

5. ***Shorter trumps longer.*** Information sticks longer in learners' minds when the content delivery segments are shorter.

6. ***Different trumps same.*** The brain pays more attention to environmental elements that change and ignores elements that are routine, repetitive, predictable, or boring.

Working The Principle: Movement Trumps Sitting

All of the exercises in this section center around one basic concept: *the longer learners sit, the less they learn.* So the major goal of the strategies and activities listed here is to get learners to move.

Below are four strategies to help you apply *Movement Trumps Sitting* to your own instruction:

► **Movement And The Ten-Minute Rule.** About every ten minutes, stop talking and have learners *do* something that includes physical movement: stand and stretch, sit and stretch, turn and talk, bend, twist, or write. Insert a *Body Break* activity after each ten-minute content segment.

► **Combine Content And Movement.** Combine physical motion with content review as often as possible. For example, while learners do a *Body Break,* they can also engage in a one-minute, paired discussion about what they've learned.

► **Hand It Over.** Tell learners why you are encouraging them to move every ten minutes, then give them opportunities to lead some of the motion-based review activities. For example, after you lead a *Body Break,* let table groups take turns leading the class in the next series of *Body Breaks.*

► **Make It Fun.** Movement can be fun as well as purposeful. A purposeful example is: *"Walk to a wall chart and write three facts you've just learned about the topic."* A fun example is: *"Stand and do two jumping jacks while telling your table group the most important fact you learned."*

Whenever smiles or laughter accompany movement, an endorphin release occurs in the brain. Endorphins are the pleasure chemicals associated with pleasant experiences. These chemicals make learning fun and, consequently, more desirable and memorable.

Five Activities That
Put The Principle To Work

On the next pages are five learning activities that primarily use *Movement Trumps Sitting*. Some activities combine this principle with others.

Place a Post-It® flag on the activity pages you plan to use in your next training.

After trying out the exercise, write field notes about how the activities worked. Suggestions for field notes are: what worked and what didn't, ways to modify or improve the activities, your summaries, comments, and activity evaluations. In effect, these field notes will become your written records for future use.

More Notes

1. Body Breaks

Body Breaks are short, quick ways for learners to get more oxygen to their brain and body while still focusing on the topic.

Use *Body Breaks* between content segments. These activities are not "official" breaks of ten or more minutes but rather one-minute oxygen-producing motions. Vary the *Body Breaks* so that you are not repeating the same ones. More importantly, create some kind of visual or auditory reminder (a timer, learner signal, Post-It® note, or the like) for yourself so that *you* will remember to stop talking and include a *Body Break*.

Duration: One minute or less.

Detailed Instructions:
Learners individually stand and stretch while thinking about what they've learned so far. At the end of about thirty seconds, give them a signal to sit down and quickly share a short summary of their thoughts with a partner or their table group.

Variations:
Follow The Leader. You lead the first *Body Break* by having learners copy a simple stretch you do. Then assign volunteers to lead the next ones. Or have each table group lead a stretch for the whole group to follow.

Stand, Stretch, And Speak. All table groups stand. One person at each table leads a stretch for his own table group. During the stretch, the leader states the most important concept he has learned so far. Each table group member takes a turn at leading a stretch and sharing a comment.

Sit, Stretch, And Speak. Instead of standing, one person at each table leads a sitting stretch while stating the most important concept learned. The other group members copy the stretch. Each member takes a turn doing this.

Bend, Breathe And Write. Learners drop a pen or pencil on the floor.

As they bend down to pick up the writing tools, they exhale forcefully so that their lungs are completely empty. As they straighten up, they inhale and take a deep breath. Then they stretch their arms up over their heads and pretend to write on the ceiling a word or phrase that describes what they think about what they are learning. They can also write this on their handout or any note-taking paper. If you wish, have them share what they wrote with a partner or their table group.

For eLearning:

Insert *Body Breaks* into the printed material, as I did on page 49. Will you know for sure if learners follow the instructions or not? Nope. However, they'll probably do the activities because you are the "teacher" and they have been conditioned to do what teachers direct them to do. Additionally, when the printed instructions describe *what* learners need to do and *why* they need to do it (as did my instructions to you), they will know the brain research behind the request.

Here are more examples of printed instructions:

▶ *After reading this paragraph, stand and stretch. Think about what you've learned. Take a few deep breaths, stretch again, then sit down and continue reading. You just increased the amount of oxygen flowing to your brain. This will enhance your ability to remember what you've learned.*

▶ *After reading this paragraph, stand up and do a few slow jumping jacks (or walk in place) while thinking about what you've learned so far. After doing the jumping jacks, write a one-sentence summary of what you thought about. Then continue reading.*

▶ *After reading these instructions, take thirty seconds to do a few stretches while seated: rotate your neck, stretch your arms over your head, bend down as if doing a seated bow, lean to one side of your chair and then the other. You are increasing the oxygen to your body and brain which will help you remember more of the content as you read.*

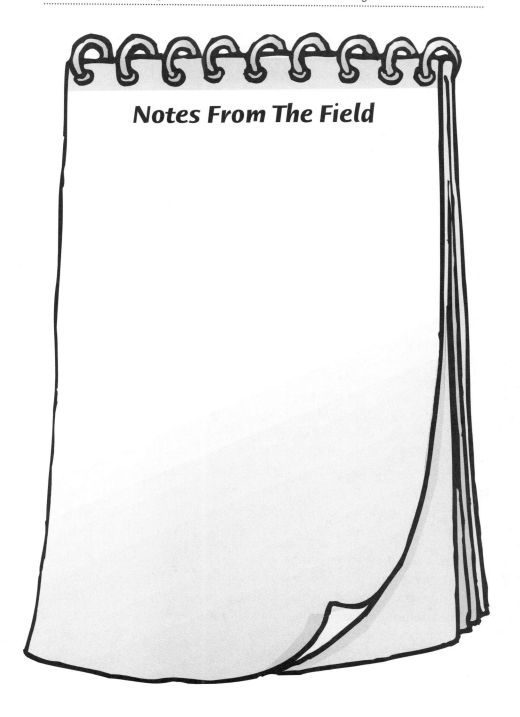

Notes From The Field

2. Walk And Talk

Also called a *Walkabout,* this activity is a more structured *Body Break*. Basically, learners take a short walk with a friend while talking about the topic.

While doing a *Walk And Talk,* learners do *one* of the following: they walk around the room, walk to one wall and back, walk around their tables, or walk to the front of the room and back. You can play upbeat music during the exercise to add rhythm and energy to the *Walk And Talk*. Use this activity to vary the *Body Break* exercises.

Duration: From one to five minutes, depending upon the size of the group and the space in which to walk.

Detailed Instructions:
Tell learners to form standing pairs or triads and to make sure no one is left out. While music plays, have them walk around the room and talk about what they've learned. They can also discuss how they plan to use the information or opinions they have about the content. When you signal that the time is up, they return to their seats. Remind learners to thank their *Walk And Talk* partners for taking a stroll with them.

Variations:
Inside, Outside. If a door to the outside is close by, learners walk outside while talking to each other. While outside, they breathe in the fresh air and do some easy stretches. Then they return to the room.

Follow The Leader Revisited. Once learners have done the first *Walk And Talk,* have them take part in the decision *when* to do another and *what* to talk about. Or, each table group can be responsible for leading a *Walk And Talk* at various times during the class.

For eLearning:
Include the instructions for a *Walk And Talk* in the printed material just like you do for a *Body Break*. If the learner has no one to

walk and talk with, she can simply walk alone and talk to herself, or just think about what she has learned. Examples of printed instructions are:

► *Walk around the room you are in while pretending to explain to a reporter what you have learned so far.*

► *Walk outside the room you are in and then back inside, while thinking about three major facts from the material.*

► *Walk around your computer chair, then sit and write a one-sentence summary of what you have learned.*

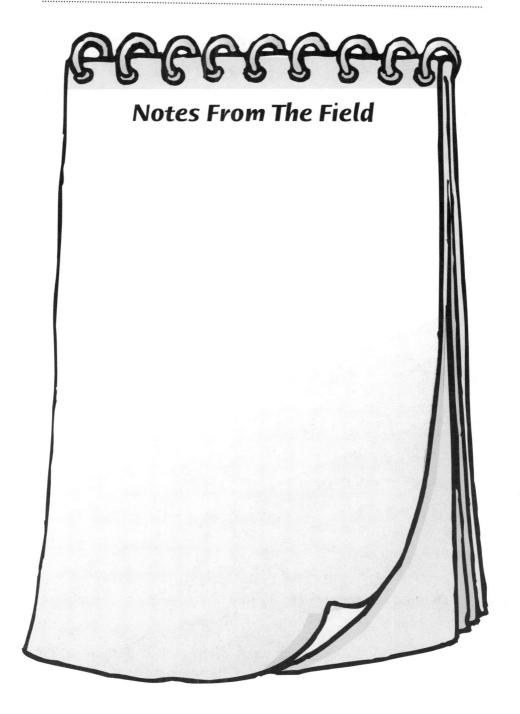

Notes From The Field

3. Wall-Writing

This activity combines movement with writing. During the exercise, learners stand and walk over to charts taped to the walls. They write topic-related responses on the charts. You can repeat *Wall-Writing* at different times for different reasons. For example, as an opening, learners write what they already know or think they know about the topic. As a review, learners write what they have just learned. As a closing, learners write how they plan to use what they've learned.

A structured *Wall-Writing* activity is when you direct learners to write specific responses on labeled charts at designated times. A more un-structured format allows learners to choose what to write and when.

Duration: From one to five minutes.

Detailed Instructions:
Tape a number of blank chart pages on the walls around the room (usually, one page for every 3 – 5 learners). At different times during the class, tell learners to stand and, with colored markers, write some-thing on one of the wall charts. You can tell them specifically what to write, or you can post a list of suggestions on a slide and give them a choice of what to write. More than one person can write on each chart at the same time. Here is an example of a list of suggestions:

- ▶ *An answer to this question (print question here)*
- ▶ *A question you still have*
- ▶ *A summary statement*
- ▶ *An opinion about the content*
- ▶ *Facts you want to remember*
- ▶ *The most important thing you've learned so far*
- ▶ *How you plan to use what you've learned*

You may decide to label each chart with a sentence starter before the class begins. Remember to *print* the labels in large letters with dark-colored markers so learners can easily read them. Examples of sentence starters are:

- *What I want to learn ...*
- *A fact I want to remember ...*
- *My opinion about this is ...*
- *I also know that ...*
- *A question I still have ...*
- *A suggestion is ...*
- *What I plan to do with this information ...*
- *I can share this information with ...*
- *My next step is ...*

During the content delivery, refer to the wall charts whenever appropriate. Allow some time before the closing for learners to walk around and read the charts. Follow this with a short, whole-group discussion about what they read and observed. At this time, you may choose to answer some of their written questions or make your own comments in response to their written statements.

Question examples to guide the whole group discussion are:

- *What surprised you?*
- *What patterns did you notice in the responses?*
- *What were some similarities and differences between what you wrote and what others wrote?*
- *What are some comparisons you can make between what was written at the beginning of the class versus at the end?*
- *What are you taking away from this exercise?*

Variations:

Group Charts. Each table group has its own wall chart, with group members writing on the same chart throughout the class. After the class, collect the charts, take a photo of each, and email the photos to the class as "souvenirs" of the learning. Or, assign the photo-taking to a volunteer.

Table-Writing. Place a labeled chart paper and colored markers on each table top. When directed to do so, learners stand and move from table to table, writing on each chart. Or they stand, switch tables, write on one chart, then return to their own table and read what others have written.

For eLearning:

The learner creates his own wall chart by taping a piece of chart paper (or large sheet of printer paper) to a wall in the room in which he is studying. When the printed instructions direct him to do so, he stops reading, stands and writes on the chart paper. In the printed instructions, remember to explain *why* standing up is important. Examples of printed instructions are:

▶ *Stand and write one outcome you hope to get from this course. Standing up increases oxygen to your brain and will help you learn and remember the content better than if you just remain seated.*

▶ *Stand and write one question you want answered.*

▶ *Stand and write one important fact you've learned about this topic so far.*

▶ *Write what you think an answer might be to the question you wrote earlier.*

▶ *Write one thing you plan to do with this information.*

▶ *Write what your next step will be after you finish this course.*

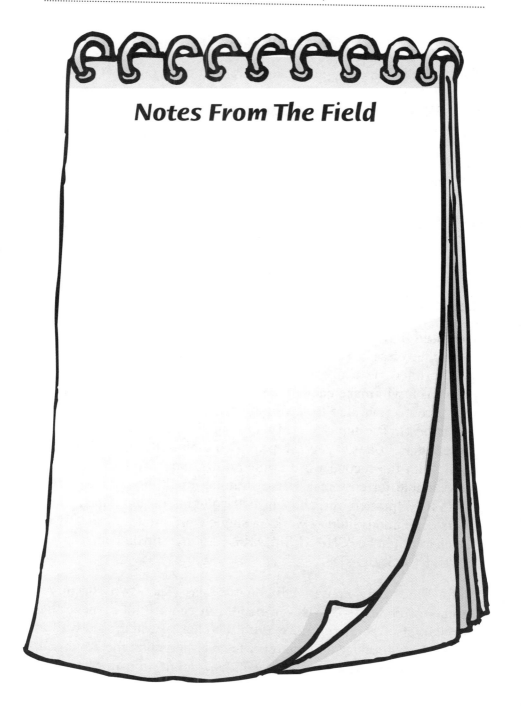

Notes From The Field

4. Review Relay

This activity is a competitive, topic-related relay race that makes a great closing exercise for a half-day or full-day training. Teams compete against each other and the team that first completes its chart wins the relay.

The *Review Relay* works best when there is plenty of space and a direct line from each team to its respective wall chart. But, even with the interference of desks and tables, the activity can be done, albeit more carefully. If fast walking is difficult for a learner, allow that person the right to pass or give him a different job to do (passing the marker, verbally encouraging the teams, holding and awarding the prizes).

Duration: From ten to fifteen minutes.

Detailed Instructions:
Before the class begins, create a one-page chart with a topic-related word printed vertically, in large letters, down the left side of the paper. You will make enough copies of this chart for the number of relay groups you plan to have (about 5 – 7 people per relay team works best). The topic-related word should have at least seven or more letters in it. Or you can print two topic-related words on the chart, with the second word printed down the middle of the page. An example for customer service training might be "CUSTOMER SERVICE" printed vertically in two columns on the paper. For a course on famous literary works, a single word printed vertically on the chart might be "SHAKESPEARE." An investment course might be "STOCKS, BONDS."

Before the relay activity, divide the class into two (or more) groups of about five to seven people in each. Find a space that is relatively free of furniture, with the charts posted on a wall at one end of the space and the relay teams lined up at the other end, one team per chart page. Each team has one fat, felt-tipped, dark-colored marker. Teams will pass this marker from team member to team member.

Give the groups about a minute to brainstorm all the topic-related words or phrases that begin with any of the letters on the chart. When you say "Go!" each team sends a member (walking fast, not running) to its respective chart to write the word or phrase that begins with one of the letters on the chart. That person returns to his team and passes the marker to another team member. Each person on the team must take a turn walking and writing before team members can repeat a turn. Team members must write a different word/phrase for each letter, even if the letter is a repetition of a previous letter. They do not have to write the words/phrases in the order of the letters. The team that first completes all the letters on its chart wins the relay.

Encourage teams to cheer for each other and to applaud the winning team. You can also designate first place, second place, third place, and so on. If you wish, award small toy prizes for the winning team and consolation prizes for the others.

Variations:

Writing Brainstorm. Before the relay, in addition to brainstorming all the topic-related words to use, team members write the words on individual index cards and use these notes during the relay race.

Outdoor Relay. If there is enough space outside, and a building wall (or sufficient chart stands) on which to hang the charts, by all means take the activity outdoors. It will add to the enthusiasm and excitement.

Sitting Relay. If there is no room for an actual relay race, learners remain seated and pass team papers from member to member instead. Before the relay, have each team vertically print designated topic-related words on its paper. When the relay begins, team members take turns writing on the team paper and passing it to the next team member until one team has finished all the writing.

For eLearning:

If there are two or more learners who are participating in some form of synchronous learning, and who are in the same room, have each learner make his own relay race paper with the designated words. Then they compete against each other using the individual pages. This is similar to the written version of *Beat-The-Clock* on page 232.

Consider using a different activity instead of this one if the elearning is asynchronuous (self-study).

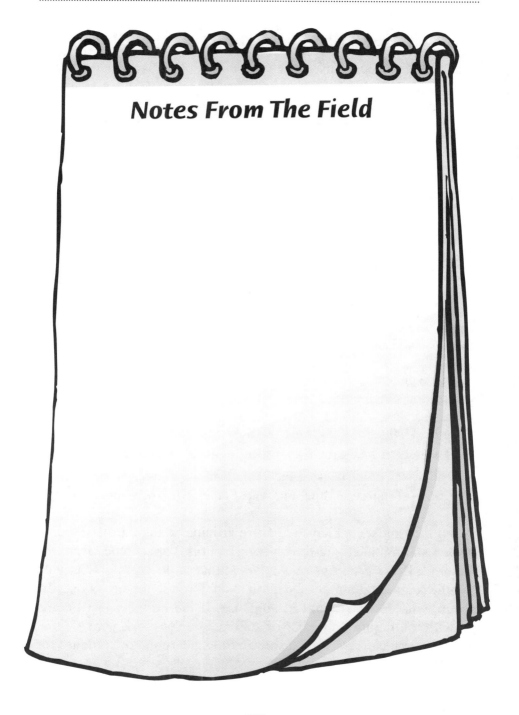

Notes From The Field

5. Beat-The-Clock (moving version)

Also called *Pop-Ups*, this activity is a competition between the whole group and the clock. Like *Review Relay, Beat-The-Clock* is an excellent closing activity because it generates engagement, enthusiasm, and positive energy that learners take with them when they leave.

Another option is to conduct this activity after an especially intense content segment. Or, use this activity more than once between content segments, changing it a bit each time.

Duration: One or two minutes.

Detailed Instructions:
Ask for a volunteer to be the timekeeper. Have the group decide how many different statements about the topic have to be made in one minute. A good rule of thumb is about fifteen to twenty statements, depending upon the complexity of the topic.

Assign a person to count the *Beat-The-Clock* statements. The counter accepts the statements if:

▶ The person speaking is standing up.

▶ The person speaking is *not* repeating what someone else has said.

▶ No two people speak at the same time. If more than one person stands at the same time, they must take turns speaking.

When the timekeeper says to start, participants take turns standing up and stating one topic-related word, phrase, or sentence from the material. If the group *beats the clock*, that is, learners collectively say the required number of statements before the time runs out, the group wins. Lead a round of applause. If the group doesn't come up with the required number of statements, the clock wins. If that happens, you can repeat the exercise or lead a round of applause for the effort.

Variations:

There are other *Beat-The-Clock* variations in the following sections: *Talking Trumps Listening, Images Trump Words,* and *Writing Trumps Reading.*

For eLearning:

Use the other variations for this activity instead of the moving version. The drawing, talking, and writing variations are more practical for elearning.

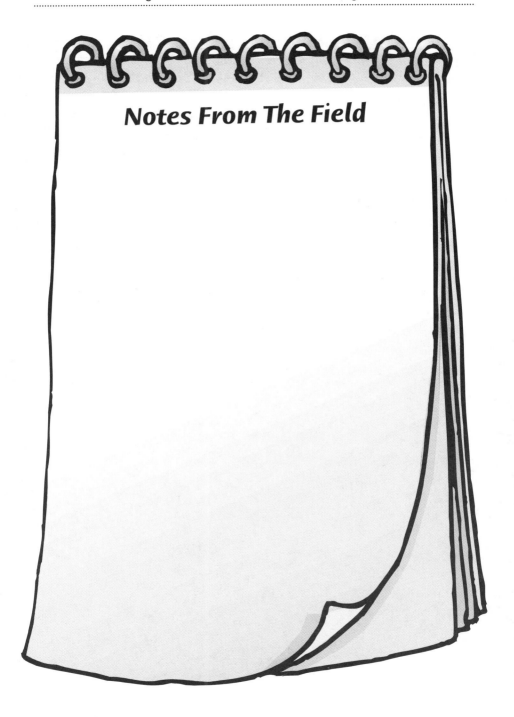

Notes From The Field

Working The Principle: Talking Trumps Listening

The basic concept that underlies the exercises in this section is: *learners understand and remember more when they talk about what they are learning.*

Listed below are five strategies to help you apply *Talking Trumps Listening:*

▶ **Stop Talking**. This may be the most challenging thing to do, since you probably have a large quantity of information to cover. Just remember: the longer you talk, the less they learn. You only need to stop talking for a minute or so—just enough time to give your learners sixty seconds to think about and summarize what you've said.

▶ **From Low-Risk To High-Risk**. For learners, a low-risk activity is one in which they collaborate in order to answer questions. High-risk activities are ones in which learners have to individually answer questions in front of their peer group. The risk is psychological: most learners do not wish to appear ignorant in front of others.

Paired or small group responses are always more low-risk than individual responses. So begin with low-risk discussions before you more to more high-risk, one-person responses.

▶ **From Small Group To Large Group**. The math is simple. When you ask the large group a question, one person usually answers, and everyone else sits and listens. When you encourage pairs, triads, or small groups to discuss the question first, everyone gets involved in answering the question.

► **Two Before You**. Often, when a learner asks you a question, other learners know the answer. Ask for two responses to the question before you give your answer. Or ask a question and then say, "We need two (or more) responses before continuing." Obviously, you wouldn't use this strategy if there is only one right answer.

► **Make It Open-Ended**. Questions or discussion topics that challenge the brain are far more interesting than simple "yes/no, right/wrong, agree/disagree" responses. Here are a few examples of open-ended questions or discussion instructions:

   * *How does this information compare with what you already know about this topic?*

   * *What are three facts you know now that you didn't know before you came to this class?*

   * *What are two changes you can make as a result of learning this information?*

   * *Describe a benefit or challenge that you might experience as a result of using this information at work.*

   * *Compare or contrast what you know now about the topic with what you knew before the class began.*

   * *Discuss how you would explain this information to an interested co-worker or colleague.*

Five Activities That
Put The Principle To Work

On the next few pages are five activities that primarily use *Talking Trumps Listening*. Of course, some activities combine this principle with others.

Place Post-It® flags on the activity pages you decide to use. Write your field notes about what worked, what didn't work, and how you could make the activity work better in the future. Refer to your notes the next time you use these activities.

More Notes

❑ ❑ ❑ ❑ ❑ ❑ ❑

1. Turn And Talk

I also call this activity a *Pair-Share, Neighbor Nudge*, or *Dyad Dialog*. Other instructors simply call it a paired discussion.

This is the easiest and most low-risk way of engaging learners, even the reluctant ones. Learners form seated or standing pairs or triads and spend about a minute discussing the content they just learned. If you wish, you can give them a specific question to answer. After the minute ends, you resume the content delivery. Vary the activity each time you use it so that it doesn't become predictable.

Duration: One or two minutes.

Detailed Instructions:
Stop talking and direct learners to turn to someone seated close to them. Tell them to make sure no one is left out. Then say one of the following statements:

▶ *Tell your partner what you would say about this information if a newspaper reporter wanted to quote you.*

▶ *Take one minute to discuss two facts you just learned that you didn't know before.*

▶ *In one minute, talk about how you might apply this information to your job.*

▶ *Spend a minute discussing the most important concept you learned from this lecture.*

▶ *With your partner, take a minute to create an exam question about what we've covered. You will share your question with the class.*

▶ *Tell your neighbor how you plan to use what you've learned.*

If time allows, ask for a few volunteers to report a short summary of their discussion. Or, if time is short, skip the reporting and continue with the content delivery.

Variations:

Strangers To Friends. Learners stand and find someone they haven't yet talked to. Have them introduce themselves then discuss the content, or have them answer a topic-related question.

Foursomes. Learners work in pairs while hunting for specific data within the handouts or other printed material (main ideas, important facts, key words). Then they form a foursome with another pair and share what they found.

For eLearning:

If the course is synchronous and learners are attending it with others, the *Turn And Talk* works the same as if they were in a face-to-face class. Learners talk with someone in the physical room they're in, in a virtual room, or break out into electronic chat rooms.

If the course is asynchronus, learners can talk to themselves or pretend to be talking to another person. Or they can simply mentally review what they've learned then write down what they might say if asked to explain the content to someone else.

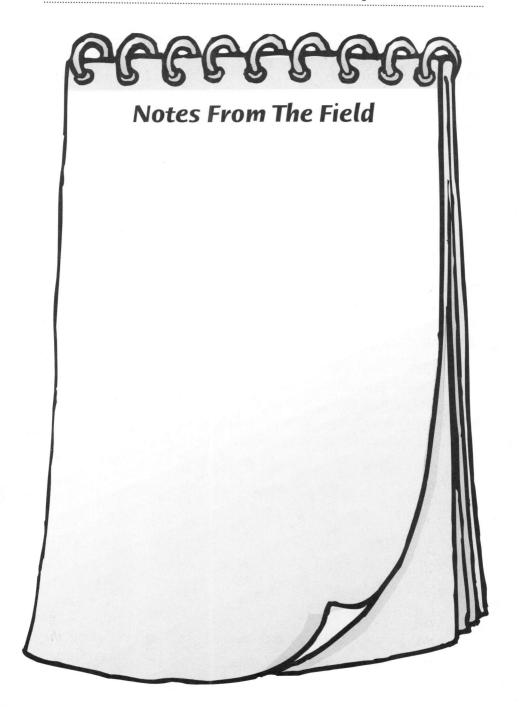

Notes From The Field

2. Standing Survey

This activity is a high-energy, low-risk way of combining movement, writing and talking. It is also an excellent opening or closing activity. As an opening exercise, learners stand and gather information others already know or think they know about the topic. As a closing exercise, they compare it to what they've learned during the class.

To add accountability to the exercise, learners report the *Standing Survey* results to their table groups immediately after the activity ends.

Duration: From five to ten minutes, depending upon the length of the small group discussions afterwards.

Detailed Instructions:

Tell learners to stand and gather specific information from other people who are *not* members of their table groups. Make sure they take a pen/pencil and index card on which to write because they will be reporting back to their table groups afterwards. Suggest a question to ask (or have one printed on a slide or chart) and tell them the activity time limit (two or three minutes, or the length of one musical piece).

Here are examples of verbal instructions for *Standing Surveys:*

▶ *Stand up and gather at least three facts about the topic from people who are __not__ sitting at your table. Write the facts on an index card and report your survey results to your table group after time is called.*

▶ *Stand up and ask two people from other groups what they already know about the topic. Write down their responses and be ready to tell your table group what was said.*

▶ *Form a standing group with two or three others who are __not__ seated at your table. In one minute, find out everything they already know about the topic. Jot down a one-sentence summary of of what each person said, then be ready to share the summary with your table group.*

▶ *Stand and ask three people from other tables what they want to learn from this class. Be ready to share their responses with the group.*

If time is short, learners can report their *Standing Survey* results later in the class. Or, ask a few volunteers to report their results to the whole group.

Variation:

Postcard Partners. Create a set of index cards with a specific, topic-related question on each card. Pass out the cards or place one on each learner's chair. There should be at least four different questions and each table should have a mixture of the questions.

During the opening, learners stand and find two or more other people who have the same question but who are not sitting at their table. They discuss the question and, together, write a short summary of the discussion on the cards. Then they return to their table groups and share their questions and answers.

To make this variation more interesting, use stickers, computer graphics, or a stamp of a picture on the front of the cards. Each question will have its own picture so learners match pictures as well as questions. Make the visuals content-related to add more meaning.

For eLearning:

Again, if the class is synchronous, learners break out into chat rooms and discuss a specific question from a list of questions they find in the printed material. If the class is asynchronous, the learner chooses one question from the list and writes an answer. Then he continues reading.

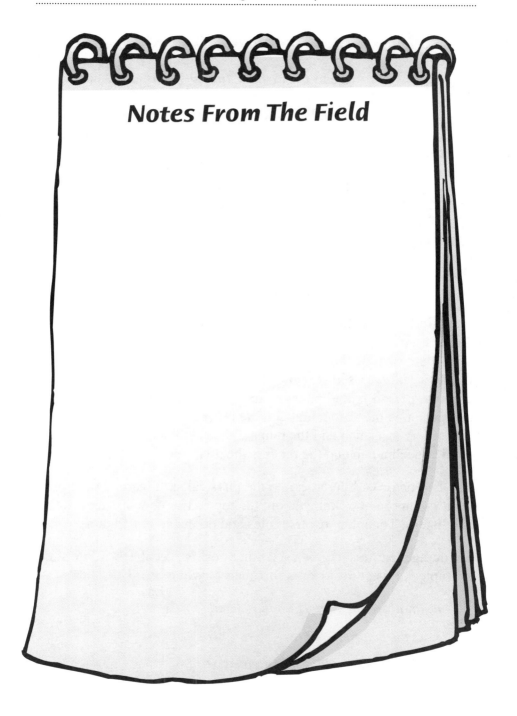

Notes From The Field

3. Each Teach

This activity is a more in-depth *Turn And Talk*. It is an excellent way for learners to demonstrate and reinforce physical skills learned during the class. If the class is more information-based, this activity becomes more of a role-play in which one learner becomes the instructor and the other pretends to be a new learner.

You can use this activity as a way to check for understanding, as well. Walk around, watch, and listen while learners teach each other. You'll get an adequate assessment of what they know and the content you need to review later.

Duration: From five to ten minutes, depending upon the skill demonstrations and whole-group discussion afterwards.

Detailed Instructions:
Tell learners to form seated or standing pairs or triads. Explain that one person will be the instructor and the other will be a new learner. Create a reality-based scenario that is related to the topic. Examples are: one person is the manager and the other is the new employee; one person is the accountant and the other is a tax client; one person is the store salesman and the other is the customer; one person is the medical technician and the other is the assistant.

The instructor will demonstrate the physical skill learned or explain what is important to know about the topic. The new learner watches and listens. Then they reverse roles and do the activity again.

Encourage learners to give each other positive feedback. Write some examples of what to say on a flip chart or white board:

► *Yes, that's really important to remember.*

► *That was helpful to know.*

► *You demonstrated that skill clearly.*

▶ *You obviously understand the concepts.*

▶ *Thank you for explaining the content so well.*

By giving learners examples of specific positive feedback, you are encouraging them to be more explicit when complimenting each other. A statement such as "I liked that" or "That was good" says nothing about *why*. A statement such as "You explained that so clearly and it was easy to understand" gives the *why* for the compliment.

Furthermore, the feedback can take the form of additional information:

▶ *You explained these concepts and you might want to add two more ...*

▶ *In addition to these skills steps, remember to do this as well ...*

▶ *A suggestion I have to add to what you already know is ...*

▶ *You might want to think about these facts in addition to what you explained to me ...*

Follow the *Each Teach* activity with a short, whole group discussion about the skill demonstrated or information shared, in order to clarify any confusion or answer further questions.

Variations:

Table Teach. Table groups volunteer to demonstrate the skill learned or to do a short presentation about the content.

Homework Teach. If the training lasts more than one day, assign a homework exercise in which learners have to teach a family member, friend, or colleague something they learned during the training. Inform the learners they will report to their table groups about the experience and the result.

For eLearning:

See the elearning suggestions for the *Turn And Talk* activity.

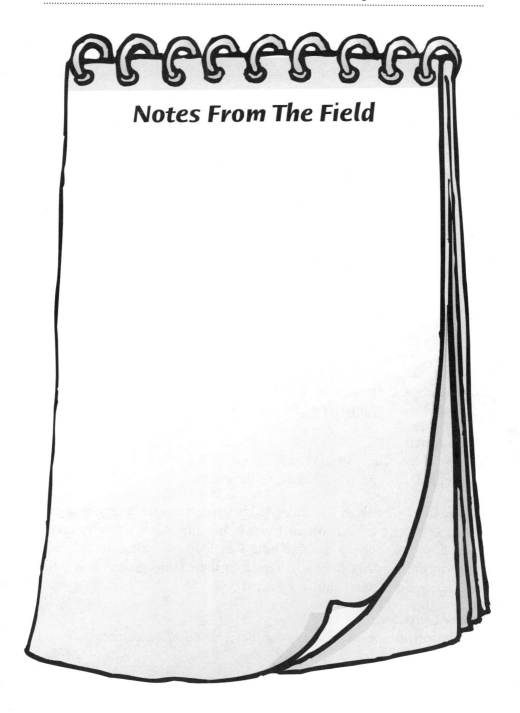

Notes From The Field

4. Talking Whip

This is an improvisational activity and a rapid-fire variation of *Each Teach*, in which each learner has one minute to stand and explain some of the content covered during the class. When one learner's sixty seconds are up, another learner takes the first one's place. The talking "whips" around the room until everyone (or a certain number of learners) has had a turn.

Duration: One minute for each participant. If the class is large, shorten each talk to thirty seconds.

Instructions:
Explain that each person will have one minute to stand and summarize what he or she learned, demonstrate a new skill, or explain how to apply the new content. The learner will continue talking until sixty seconds is up. Then she sits down and the next learner must quickly take her place, continuing where she left off or talking about another topic-related concept.

The person talking can choose the next person to take her place, or you can direct what order the learners will follow (clockwise around each table, up and down rows, etc.). You can also give the talker a small throwable object like a Koosh® or Nerf® ball. The talker throws the object to the person he decides will go next.

As mentioned above, if the class is large, shorten the talks to thirty seconds each. Or designate six talks in six minutes. Or do the *Table Whip* variation below.

If you give learners a minute or two to prepare their *Talking Whips*, they will feel more at ease with the activity. Suggest that they jot down a few notes to use, as well.

Variation:
Table Whips. If the group is large (more than twenty) it is more effective to do the *Talking Whip* within table groups. The instructions are

the same but each table group assigns a person to be the timer for the group. Each group member does her sixty-second talk in front of her table group instead of the whole class.

For eLearning:

For synchronous classes, ask for volunteers to do the *Talking Whip*. For self-study, assign this strategy for homework or choose the *Turn And Talk* exercise instead.

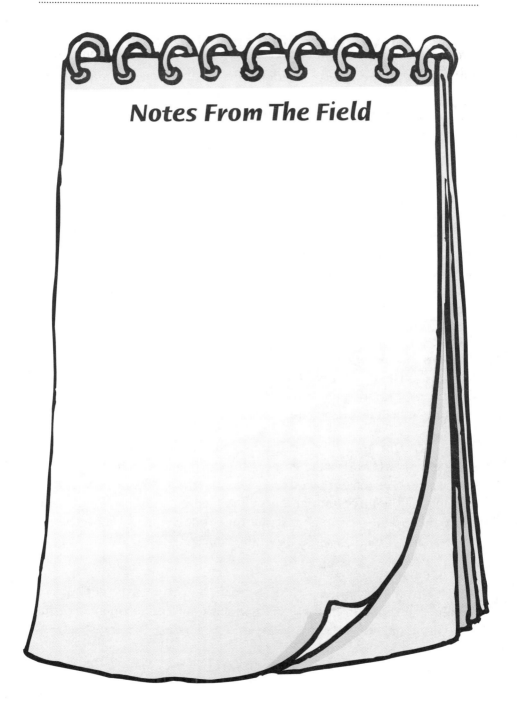

Notes From The Field

5. Beat-The-Clock (talking version)

With all *Beat-The-Clock* variations, the competition is collaborative because it is the group against the clock. Once learners understand the structure of the exercise, they can make up their own versions of this activity.

Duration: One or two minutes.

Detailed Instructions:
For this version of *Beat-The-Clock*, learners remain seated and simply shout out as many responses as they can before the pre-assigned time is up. You tell them the type of responses needed (answers to a question, topic-related facts, questions for a test) and the time limit. If the group beats the clock with a high number of responses, follow the activity with a round of applause.

Variations:
Change The Numbers. Choose a specific number of responses that learners must come up with during the time allowed. Learners take turns verbally stating one response until the number has been reached. Anyone in the class can state a fact.

Who Has The Mouth? Learners use a soft, throwable object like a Koosh® or Nerf® ball as the group's "mouth." Whoever has the mouth states a content-related fact then tosses the mouth to someone else. If they have to get a certain number of responses within a certain time limit, the tossing gets to be fast and fun. You may not want to choose this version if there are liquids on the tables.

For eLearning:
Again, for a synchronous class, learners do the activity verbally or within chat room groups. For an asynchronous course, include printed instructions for the written version of *Beat-The-Clock* instead.

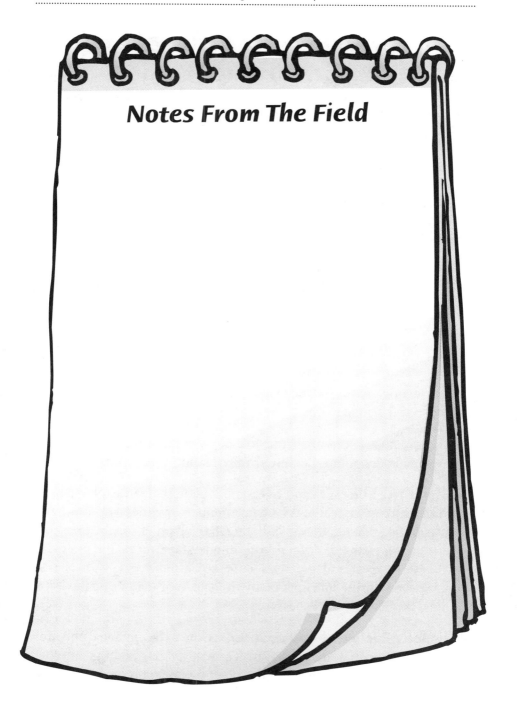

Notes From The Field

Working The Principle: Images Trump Words

In this section, the strategies and activities all revolve around one concept: *learners remember what they picture in their mind better than what they hear with their ears.*

Here are six strategies that will help you apply *Images Trump Words:*

► **Pictures In Place Of Print**. Whenever possible, use an image in place of print, especially when showing PowerPoint® slides. These should be visual representations of what you're talking about, not printed versions of your lecture material.

Get rid of the slides that have paragraphs, bulleted sentences and the tiny, impossible-to-read print. Replace the words with interesting, topic-related photos that are large enough to cover most of the screen area.

If you must use words, put *one* topic-related phrase across or alongside the photo. Lecture from your notes, not from the slides.

► **Slash The Slides**. I can't overstate it enough: learners have been slide-decked to death. Whatever number of slides you normally use, divide that number in half, then half again. Keep the ones that are image-rich and crucial to the understanding of the material. Delete the rest and put their content on handouts, wall charts, table tents (print concepts on them instead of learner names), job aids, flashcards, worksheets, etc.

► **Images For Need-To-Know Concepts**. Use images only for the concepts that are crucial to learners' understanding. In other words, use images that invoke reactions or emotions when the learners must know the information in order to do their job or to pass the test. The nice-to-know information goes elsewhere (again: handouts, job aids, worksheets, manuals, and the like).

Remember, images can be topic-related stories, case studies, vignettes, metaphors, and analogies, as well as photos.

▶ **Take The Time**. Yes, it takes time to gather visuals that are topic-related, interesting, and evoke emotion. But the time you spend doing this is well worth the payoff in terms of increasing interest, motivation, and retention.

Schedule the time to hunt for images: an hour to find a half-dozen appropriate Internet photos, fifteen minutes to sort through photos you have taken, ten minutes to make a slide with a photo you have selected. The task won't seem as overwhelming and you'll be surprised at how many visual changes to your slides you can create in small snippets of time.

▶ **Explore The Net**. There are thousands of Internet sites that offer both free and fee-based images. Do a search to find the ones that suit your needs and pocketbook. Begin by doing a search for the keywords "free images" to find some of the best.

The two that I use most often are *www.clipart.com* and *www.istockphoto.com*. With the first, you pay a time-based fee (for a week, month, six months, or a year) to download as many images as you wish during that time. For the second, you pay a per-photo fee. Both sites offer generous licensing agreements and royalty-free products, meaning that, as long as you abide by the licensing agreement, the site has taken care of the royalty arrangements with the image artists and creators.

▶ **Give It Away**. Give learners the job of creating topic-related images. See the five activities that follow this section for specific ways to do this.

Remember to explain the *why* for the exercise so that learners know there is a brain-based reason for creating visual symbols to represent important content. The point is *not* "art," but the transformation of words into something more powerful and memorable: a mental image.

Five Activities That Put The Principle To Work

The next five activities primarily apply the learning principle *Images Trump Words*. As with previous activities, many of these exercises also utilize other principles.

Flag the activities you decide to use. Write your field notes about what worked, didn't work, and how you could make the activity work better in the future.

□ □ □ □ □ □ □

1. Say It With Symbols

Use this activity when you want to expand traditional note-taking into an exercise that is visual/spatial. Insert *Say It With Symbols* into a lecture segment as a quick review, or at the end of the training as a closing activity.

Duration: One or two minutes.

Detailed Instructions:
Learners look over their notes, think about what they've learned, then create a visual symbol or representation of the main idea or concept. The symbol can be a doodle, cartoon, logo, icon, line drawing, shape, squiggle—anything that represents the information but does not contain words. If time allows, have learners explain their symbols to a partner or to their table group.

Variations:
Left Brain, Right Brain. Learners fold their note-taking paper in half. On the left side of the paper, they take notes in the traditional manner: writing phrases, sentences, and outlining. On the right side of the paper, they take notes using visual symbols to represent concepts.

Wall Chart Symbols. Combining physical movement with visual representations, learners stand and draw symbols on wall charts using colored markers. They work individually or collaboratively. They label their symbols with the concepts the images represent or verbally explain the symbols to other individuals or table groups.

Visual Exit Slips. In order to exit the room for a break, lunch, or the end of class, learners draw visual symbols on index cards or Post-It® notes. The symbols represent the most important concepts they've learned. They stick their notes on a wall chart as they leave the room, or they place the cards in a box or bag beside the door. This serves a double purpose: each learner is accountable for an exit slip and the slips give you a better understanding of what learners consider to be important.

For eLearning:

Printed instructions tell learners to draw content-related symbols on note-taking worksheets, index cards, or Post-It® notes. Include an example so learners understand what they need to do. Be sure to explain the *why* in the printed material. Examples of printed instructions are:

▶ *So that you will remember the information longer, draw a cartoon, logo, icon, or doodle that represents the main idea of this paragraph (section, chapter).*

▶ *To help you visualize this procedure, draw your own flow chart of the procedural steps.*

▶ *On an index card, draw an image that represents the major concept you have learned so far. Tape the card where you will see it so that it will be a visual reminder of the concept. Do this with the next major concept as well.*

▶ *On your worksheet, draw a doodle of what you have just learned. Label the doodle. Think about how you would explain what the doodle stands for if someone asked you about it.*

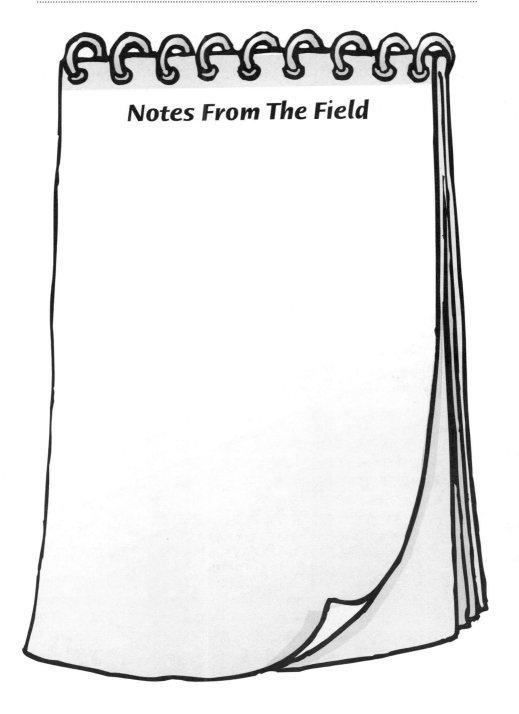

Notes From The Field

2. Mental Metaphors

Any time learners compare or contrast one thing to another, they are using metaphors (similes and analogies are types of metaphors). With *Mental Metaphors*, learners create their own metaphors to represent important concepts.

As with *Say It With Symbols,* this exercise helps learners think about the content in more visual ways to help deepen their understanding and retention of the material.

Duration: About five minutes.

Detailed Instructions:
Before the class, print the following formula on a slide or wall chart:

This (concept) is like a (blank) because: (three reasons).

Learners work in table groups. Each group chooses one concept from the content covered, one household object, and three reasons why the concept is like this household object. At the end of about two minutes, table groups share their metaphors with the whole group. Lead a round of applause for each group.

You may decide to give learners an example of a topic-related *Mental Metaphor.* Here are three examples from my training programs:

► *The POS (Point-Of-Sale) customer service procedure is like a scissors because it cuts through red tape, shapes the customer's information into easy-to-use pieces, and cuts out future mistakes.*

► *Financial planning is like a blender because you throw all the information you have into the blender, you add the ingredients (financial guidelines) that will make it stick together, and hopefully, the refreshing drink that results will be satisfying to your wallet.*

▶ *The brain science behind effective instruction is like a smooth-running engine because all the parts (principles) work together to get learners where they need to go, all parts are symbiotic (you can't have one without the other), and, if the learning breaks down, you can analyze the parts to determine what needs to be done to solve the problem.*

Variations:

Gadget Metaphors. Before the training begins, put a small box or lunch bag on each table. In each box, place a half-dozen small office or household objects (examples: a stapler, small toy, pencil sharpener, spoon, paperclip, whisk, screwdriver, whistle, sponge, baseball, nail, bar of soap, glue, small stuffed animal, paper cup, scissors, etc.). After a lecture segment, each table group chooses an item from its box and creates a *Mental Metaphor* using the item and the metaphor formula. If time allows, groups can volunteer to share their metaphors with the whole class.

Wall Chart Metaphors. Like the activity *Wall Chart Symbols,* table groups draw their metaphors on wall charts using colored markers. Afterwards, they share their metaphors with the whole class.

For eLearning:

Print the metaphor instructions and include a space for learners to either type their metaphors on-screen or write them on a pre-printed handout.

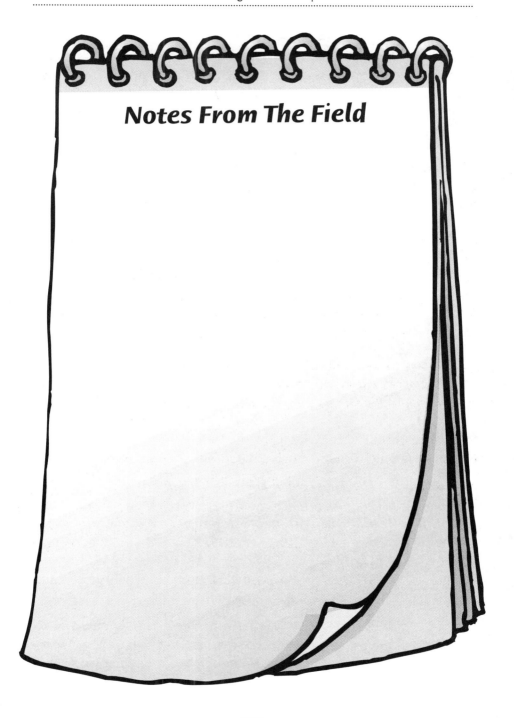

Notes From The Field

3. Story Starters

Use this activity when you want learners to create their own real-life scenarios to illustrate their understanding of the content. They can add to or alter their stories later, after they have learned more information.

Duration: One or two minutes for each story segment; five minutes to share stories at the end of the activity.

Detailed Instructions:
After a lecture segment, begin a topic-related story, real-life scenario, or case study pertaining to the lecture content. I'll use a customer service call center example as an illustration.

▶ *Call center example: A customer calls, wanting to speak to the manager of the company.*

Tell table groups to add a problem or challenge to the story.

▶ *Example: The customer has a complaint about a computer she purchased.*

Continue the next lecture segment, then tell table groups to brainstorm the next step in their story, using the information from the lecture.

▶ *Example: The call center employee listens to the complaints, apologizes for the problem, and then paraphrases what he has heard. He asks the customer if his summary of the problem is correct.*

Continue the rest of the lecture segments, alternating between content (you) and the story line (table groups).

▶ *Example: The call center offers the customer four options: to make an appointment for a technology expert to go to the customer's house and fix the computer, if possible; to take the computer to a local, licensed store to get it fixed; to send the computer to the technology department at the regional store; to return the computer for replacement or refund.*

Of course, the lecture segments will contain the information table groups need to create correct solutions to their stories. At the end of the exercise, each group verbally shares its story with the class.

Variations:

Pass The Story. Each table group creates the beginning of a topic-related story. The group writes it on a sheet of paper, then passes the paper to another table group. During the second round, the second group continues the story then passes the paper to another group. During the third round, the next group adds another piece to the story.

Each time the groups pass their papers, the new groups continue the stories using the content from the class. Finally, the papers are returned to their original groups who finish their stories and read them aloud to the class. The goal of the entire exercise is to give learners opportunities to illustrate their understanding of the content with real-life stories co-created by multi-groups.

Branching Stories. Much like the printed branching stories in Part Two, you first show a slide that has a story-starter printed on it. The next slide shows two or three possible responses to the story starter. Each table group chooses one of the responses then writes what might happen if this response is chosen. They read their scenarios to the class.

Here is an automotive workshop example:

▶ *Slide #1: There is a knocking sound in the engine when the driver accelerates the car. Choose one possible cause from the next slide then describe the automotive work it entails along with any other considerations.*

▶ *Slide #2:*
  1. Fuel detonation problem.
  2. Valve train problem.
  3. Connecting rod malfunction.

Each table group chooses one of the three possible causes of the problem and write its responses. Examples:

1. *Fuel detonation problem. Adjust the ignition timing. This isn't expensive and doesn't require much time to perform.*

2. *Valve train problem. Pull valve covers off and check for valve response. This is an expensive procedure that requires time and experience.*

3. *Connecting rod malfunction. Check compression, find problem, and possibly pull engine heads off or pull off the oil pan to check tolerances on connecting rods. This is complicated, expensive, and time-consuming.*

In the example above, the automotive instructor might continue the story using one of the table group's responses. Or she creates another version of the story with three more responses. The point in *Branching Stories* is to use real-life scenarios to teach concepts. The learners take part in the creation of the reality-based stories.

Branching Improvs. This activity is similar to the one above. With a *Branching Improv,* one table group creates the opening "improvisation" which is a topic-related skit akin to a role-play only with the parts already agreed upon and scripted. The group stops the improv at a critical point, turns to the class and asks what should come next. The group gives the class two possible choices, one more appropriate than the other. The class chooses, the group acts out the choice, and then the group tells the class whether or not its choice was the better one. At this point, the *Branching Improv* either continues with a sequel or stops. Alternatively, a different group takes the place of the first one with a different, topic-related improv.

For eLearning:

Branching Stories are excellent ways to structure computer-based learning. There are many variations. Some are simple to create; others are more complicated. You can explore options by doing an Internet search for "branching stories." Clark Aldrich's book *Learning by Doing* (2005) is also an excellent resource.

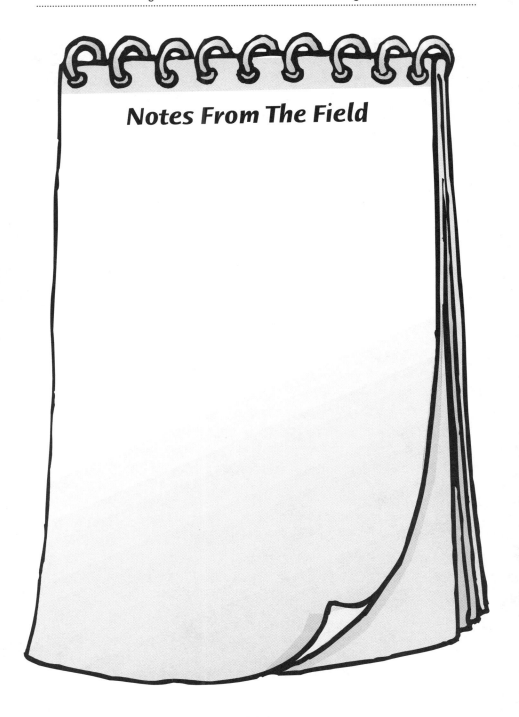

Notes From The Field

4. Memory Maps

Also called *Graphic Organizers, Mind-Maps,* or *Concept Maps, Memory Maps* are visual note-taking tools. Learners combine words with images to create more memorable written information. As with *Say It With Symbols,* learners use *Memory Maps* in place of, or in addition to, more traditional note-taking methods.

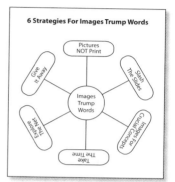

The basic *Memory Map* has a large shape (circle or square) in the middle of the paper for the topic, and smaller shapes around it for the supporting concepts or details. The smaller shapes are linked to each other or to the larger shape with lines. The lines signify the relationships between the smaller and the larger shapes.

Memory Maps can take many forms. Do an Internet search for "graphic organizers, concept maps, mind maps" and you'll find hundreds of both free and fee-based graphic organizers online, including software downloads for computer-generated mapping. Some of the graphic organizers you find will be for elementary and secondary education, but you can modify many of them for adult use.

Duration: A minute or less, each time the learner adds to his *Memory Map.*

Instructions: Before the class begins, create and hand out a simple, visual note-taking page that learners fill in during the content delivery.

Explain that learners should fill in the *Memory Map* shapes to help them remember the content better. Once the class begins, pause during or between lecture segments to give learners time to fill in their maps. At first, tell them to write main ideas and supporting facts or details. After they get used to this method of note-taking, encourage them to create their own *Memory Maps.*

Variations:

Cornell Notes. This is a specific type of graphic organizer now used by many colleges. Do an Internet search for "Cornell Notes" to find free templates of this note-taking tool. Suggest that learners use markers to color-code information, to emphasize major concepts, or to mark facts that will be on the exam.

Placemat Writing. Have learners create their own *Memory Maps* on paper placemats instead of standard printing paper. Have *Mark-Up* materials available to make the map creation more visually appealing.

Bag Writing. Do the same as *Placemat Writing,* only use paper lunch bags instead of placemats. You can find small, colored paper bags at craft stores, as well as most thrift stores. The non-glossy ones work best for note-taking (marker ink smears on the glossy bags). Learners can fill the bags with other note-taking materials used during the training: Post-It® notes, index cards, and the like.

For eLearning:

Create a downloadable printed *Memory Map* for the learner to use. In the printed content of the computer-based course, include periodic instructions for using the *Memory Map.* Examples are:

▶ *On your <u>Memory Map</u>, write the topic in the middle circle. Then write three supporting concepts in three smaller circles.*

▶ *Stop reading and write three facts related to one of the concepts on your <u>Memory Map</u>.*

▶ *Read what you've written on your <u>Memory Map</u> so far. Then add four supporting details to any of the concepts.*

▶ *Review your <u>Memory Map</u> and write a summary sentence of what you've learned across the bottom of the page.*

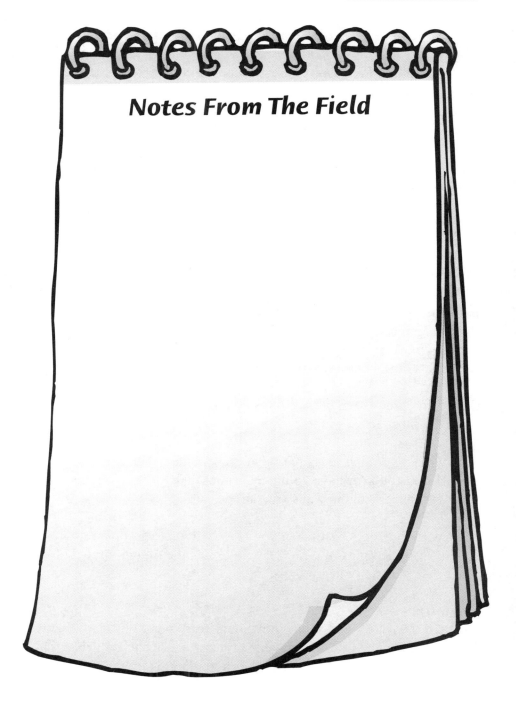

Notes From The Field

5. Beat-The-Clock (drawing version)

As with other *Beat-The-Clock* versions, learners compete against time. In this case, it probably works better to have small groups work together to beat the clock, rather than as individuals or the group as a whole.

If you choose to add another level of competition, have small groups compete against each other within the time allowed.

Duration: Up to five minutes.

Detailed Instructions:
Give each table group a sheet of chart paper and colored markers. Explain that the goal of *Beat-The-Clock* is to see how many topic-related images, symbols, or doodles each table group can create within the designated time (usually, about two or three minutes is best). The images must represent concepts learned so far. Group members can all draw at the same time to create the images.

When the time is up, table groups count their images and the group with the most gets a round of applause.

The winning group holds up its chart paper and explains its images to the whole group. Or have volunteer groups take turns doing this. Post the chart papers on the walls when done.

This activity works best when you give each table group a minute to brainstorm the kinds of topic-related visuals they might draw before the activity actually begins.

Variations:
Graffiti Time. To add more movement to this activity, tape blank chart pages on the walls. Each table group chooses one wall chart and stands by it. Each group member has a marker. After a minute or so

of brainstorming, start the activity. Group members all draw at once. The activity continues as per original instructions above.

Stick 'Em Up. Table group members draw their topic-related images on Post-It® notes. When the time is up, they stick their notes on a wall in a group cluster or on wall charts. Then they count their images. The group with the most Post-It® note images wins a round of applause.

For eLearning:
In the printed instructions for a drawing exercise, explain *why* drawing images or symbols to represent concepts helps the brain retain the information. Direct learners to use computer drawing tools or pen/paper. Or you can create a downloadable, printable note-taking page that has space for the drawings on it.

Examples of printed instructions are:

▶ *When you use pictures (images, symbols, doodles, icons) to represent main ideas, you will remember this information longer. Think about how you might represent the main ideas with pictures instead of words. Time yourself: In one minute, draw as many content-related images as you can. At the end of sixty seconds, stop drawing. Then label the images with the concepts they represent and tape them to a wall, your computer, or bulletin board. The images will remind you of what you've learned so far.*

▶ *So that you will remember more of this content, take a minute right now to convert some of the facts to pictures. On a piece of paper, draw a few images that represent important facts. The images can be doodles, icons, cartoons, or symbols. See how many pictures you can create in two minutes. Post them where you'll be reminded of what you've learned. Then continue reading.*

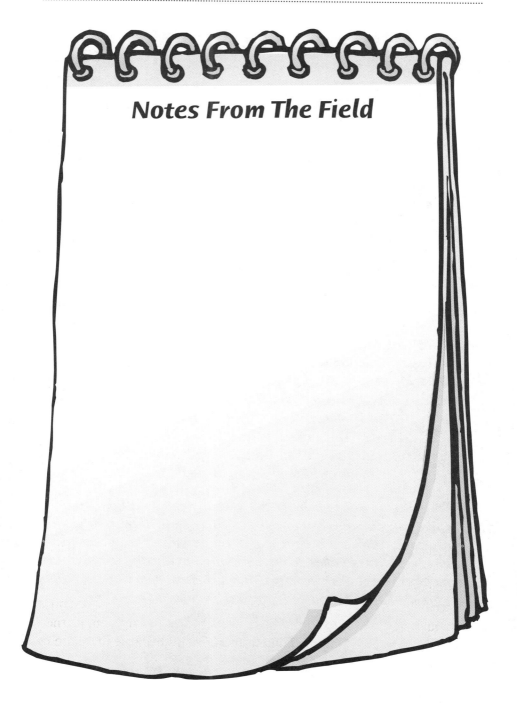

Notes From The Field

Working The Principle:
Writing Trumps Reading

When using the exercises in this section, the important concept to remember is: *writing engages more of the senses than reading alone.*

Here are six strategies to assist you when applying the principle *Writing Trumps Reading:*

► **Your Silence Is Golden.** Remind learners to write, and tell them why note-taking is an important part of learning. Then *stop talking* and give them time to write, even if it's only for thirty to sixty seconds. In one minute, they can write a content-related fact, phrase, sentence, summary, question, opinion, comment, or action plan.

Can't remember to stop talking? *Write a reminder* in your lecture notes, on a slide, or on a Post-It® note that you stick to your lecture notes, your computer, the LCD projector or your clothes (just kidding about clothes, but you get the point).

► **Give It Away Again.** Give learners the writing assignments you would ordinarily do. For example, whenever you need to write on chart paper or a smart board or white board, ask for a volunteer to do your writing for you.

When you lead a group discussion or brainstorming activity, ask for two volunteers to write on two charts. Alternate between charts so that the whole group doesn't have to wait for one volunteer to finish writing. The brainstorming pace increases this way. Furthermore, you don't have to turn your back to the group. In addition, learners will stay focused on the content more easily because there are no long pauses between brainstorming and writing.

Remember to tell the volunteers to print in large letters (using dark-colored markers, if printing on chart paper) so their writing can be read by the rest of the class.

▶ **Be Specific**. Don't say "Take some notes now." Instead, give learner specific instructions for a short, quick writing exercise. Learners will be more willing to write if they know exactly *what* they are supposed to write. Examples:

* *Write a one-sentence summary of what you have learned so far.*

* *Write three important facts you want to remember from the information you just heard.*

* *Compare what you knew when the class first began to what you know now and write a short summary of the comparison.*

* *Write your opinion about this topic: do you agree or disagree, and why or why not?*

* *Write a question you still have about this information, or one you would ask the class if you were the instructor.*

* *In sixty seconds, write as many facts about this topic as you can remember.*

If there is enough time, you might choose to lead a group discussion regarding the opinions, questions, or facts learners have written.

▶ **Blanks Are Beautiful**. Leave out important words on your slides, worksheets, or other handout material. When you get to those pieces of the content, tell your learners to fill in the blank spaces. Then give them a few seconds to do so.

▶ **Vary The Places, Spaces And Times**. Remember, the human brain usually notices *anything* in the environment that changes. It ignores anything that is routine, repetitive, or predictable. So vary the places learners take notes—places and spaces both on the page and in the room. Examples:

* *Write this fact across the top of the page.*

* *Write this bulleted point in the margin of your handout.*

* *Stand and write two important facts on the wall chart closest to your table group.*

* *Write a one-sentence summary on a Post-It® note then stick it on the cover page of your handout.*

* *Draw a circle and, inside it, write a question you still have. Draw a box and, inside it, write something you've just learned that you didn't know before.*

* *On an index card, write a short paragraph explaining to a friend what you've learned.*

Also vary the times you give specific writing instructions: at the beginning of a lecture segment, during the middle, at the end, as a review, before or after a scheduled break and/or at the opening or closing of the training.

Five Activities That
Put The Principle To Work

The next five activities primarily use *Writing Trumps Reading*. As with previous activities, many of them also incorporate other principles.

Flag the activities you decide to use, then write your field notes after you have used the activities in your own training.

□ □ □ □ □ □ □

1. Mark-Ups

Mark-Ups are all the ways learners can interact with printed material. When learners have to mark up text in a specific way, they pay more attention to what they are reading.

Mark-Ups can be as simple as highlighting certain words or phrases. They can be more complex such as hunting for the main idea in a section of printed material, then circling it and sharing what they found with others.

Duration: From ten seconds to two minutes.

Detailed Instructions:
Before the class begins, place a variety of *Mark-Up* materials on the tables: pens, pencils, highlighters, colored markers, Post-It® notes and Post-It® flags, index cards, stickers, colored dots, and the like.

If the room has individual desks, put the materials in containers that learners can pass around. Tell learners to choose some *Mark-Up* materials from the containers to use for the duration of the class. Remember to collect the materials before learners leave for re-use.

Tell learners they will be marking up the printed information in various ways: highlighting main ideas, writing comments, circling or boxing sentences or paragraphs, etc. They'll use Post-It® notes to flag important sections. They'll put dots or stickers beside the facts they want to remember. Let them know why they will be doing these *Mark-Ups*.

During the class, stop to give specific *Mark-Up* instructions. Examples:

► *Highlight the main idea on this worksheet.*
► *Circle three important facts on this page.*
► *Find the most important concept in this section and draw a box around it.*

▶ *Put a colored dot beside the action idea you will use after the class is over.*

▶ *Underline the sentence that summarizes what you just heard in the lecture.*

▶ *Flag this page with a Post-It® note so you can refer to it later.*

▶ *Write a one-sentence summary on a Post-It® note and stick it to this page.*

▶ *Write a one-sentence opinion (question, summary, or comment) about this material in the margin of the page.*

▶ *Find what you think is the most important idea on this page. Circle it. Compare what you circled with what your neighbor circled. If they are different, each of you explain why you circled what you did.*

▶ *Put stickers or colored dots beside three ideas you can use. Then pair up with someone from another table and compare ideas.*

Variations:
Make up your own *Mark-Ups,* or have learners make up theirs.

See *Dot-Voting* on page 241 and *Learner's Toolbox* on page 249 for two other variations.

For eLearning:
At the beginning of the course, give learners a printed list of suggested writing materials to have available: pen/pencil, colored markers, highlighter, Post-It® notes. You won't know if they actually use these materials, but the odds increase that they will because the list is part of the course instructions.

Make sure you insert specific, printed reminders for them to use the *Mark-Up* materials throughout the course. Examples of printed instructions are:

▶ *Stop reading now and highlight the major ideas on this page of your printed text.*

▶ *Stop reading, think about what you've learned, and write three facts about it. Highlight the most important fact.*

▶ *Look over your handout page of supporting information and circle the main ideas.*

▶ *On the handout page, use a marker to draw a colored box around the procedural steps to follow.*

▶ *Write a one-sentence summary of this material on a Post-It® note then place it in your manual.*

▶ *Write your own summary of this section, then flag it with a Post-It® note to make it easy to find.*

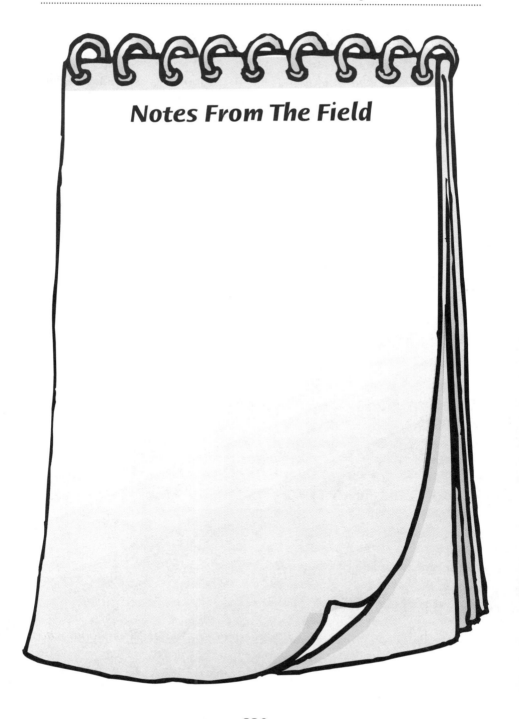

Notes From The Field

2. Quick Writes

This activity is also called a *Think And Write* or *Rapid Reflection*. It is an excellent one to combine with many of the other learning principles, especially *Talking Trumps Listening*. With it, learners pause to think about what they've learned and then write something specific about it. They can choose what to write or you can give them a specific writing assignment.

Quick Writes are excellent activities to begin and end a training session, to review a content segment, or to check for understanding.

Duration: From ten seconds to one minute.

Detailed Instructions:

Instruct learners as to what to write, where, and when. Your instructions can be verbal, visual, or a combination of both. Here are some examples:

▶ Instructions on a slide at the beginning of class: *After reading this, write what you want to learn from this class on an index card. Be ready to share this information with your table group.*

▶ Instructions on a slide at the end of class: *Think about what you've learned. On a Post-It® note, write a one-sentence summary and stick it to the door as you leave.*

▶ Instructions on a chart: *Write two facts you now know about this topic that you didn't know before.*

▶ Instructions on a white board: *After reading this, write your answer to the following question on this white board: "How do you plan to use this information?" Be ready to let your table group know what you wrote.*

▶ Verbal instructions at the beginning of training: *Think about what you want to learn during this training. On your handout, write your own personal learning goal. You'll come back to it later.*

- ▶ Verbal instructions at the end of training: *Think about what you've learned here. On an index card, write a summary of what was most important to you. Take this summary with you and post it somewhere visible where you'll see it and read it.*

- ▶ Verbal instructions for review: *Now, in your own words, quickly write the main idea from this section.*

- ▶ Slide instructions for review: *What question do you still have? Write it on a Post-It® note and put it on the Q&A chart.*

For eLearning:

Instruct learners to read a paragraph and then write a one-sentence summary of the main idea. Leave space for them to do so in the hand-out materials. Again, you won't know if they follow your written instructions, but they probably will, especially if you remind them that they'll remember the information longer if they stop to summarize it in their own words.

Most of the printed examples listed above will also work for elearning.

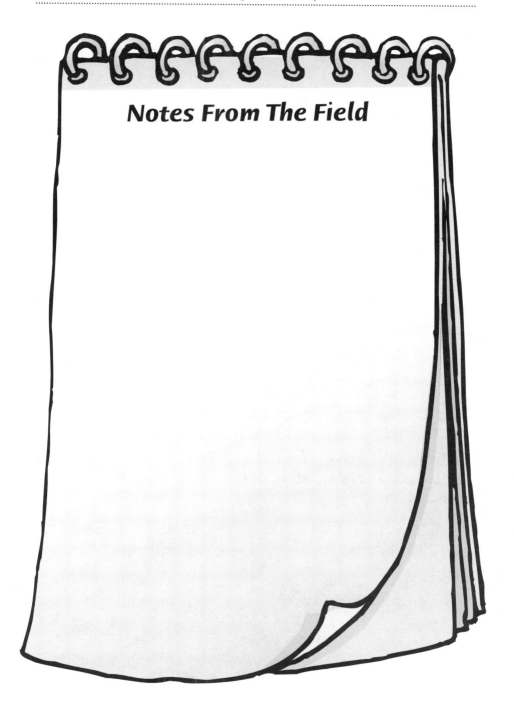

Notes From The Field

3. Three-Card-Draw

This activity is a new way of using index cards as note-taking tools. It is also a way to "bracket" the learning experience, that is, to use the same activity to open, review, and close the training. Each time learners do the exercise, they write different answers on the cards. So the activity actually changes with each use.

The *Three-Card-Draw* goes well with a card-playing theme or metaphor, although you can apply it to any learning experience, even if it is not theme-based.

Duration: About one minute per repetition.

Detailed Instructions:
Before the training, print the following on a slide, chart paper, white board, or worksheet:

▶ **Card #1: What?** *What have you learned learned about the topic?*

▶ **Card #2: So What?** *Why is this information important to you?*

▶ **Card #3: Now What?** *What is one way you might use this information?*

Place a stack of index cards on each table for the small groups to use. Or pass a card stack around the room and tell learners to each take three cards.

On the first, learners write "What?" On the second, they write "So what?" On the third, they write "Now what?"

Tell learners to keep the cards handy because they will be writing on them throughout the class. After each content segment, give learners time to fill out the cards. Ask a few volunteers to share what they wrote. Or have learners pair up and share their cards with another person. Add movement to the activity by having them stand and share cards with someone from another table group.

If learners have no more writing room on the front of the cards, have them continue writing on the back or give them more cards. Be sure to repeat the exercise one last time during the closing.

Before they leave, tell learners to take their cards with them and post them somewhere in their workspace where they will be reminded of what they learned and what they intend to do with the information.

Besides these suggestions, other possible labels for the card are: facts, opinions, comments, questions, major ideas, details, summary statements, uses, etc.

Variations:

Eight-Square Bingo. This is a variation of *Blackout Bingo.* Learners fold a blank piece of standard printer paper to make eight squares. You post a list of content-related words, phrases, or concepts on a chart or slide—items that you will cover during the training. There should be at least a dozen items listed. Each learner chooses items from the list and writes them, one per square, on his bingo paper. Learners choose items based on what they think look interesting, or what they want to learn more about. Each learner's bingo sheet will have different items in different squares.

During the content delivery, and whenever you cover one of the items on the list, those learners with that item on their bingo sheets will cross it out. The first person who crosses out all his items shouts "Bingo!" and receives a round of applause from the whole group. There can be many bingos during the training. Of course, the object is to have all learners shout "Bingo!" at some point because you will have covered all of the items on the list.

For eLearning:

The activity is the same, but with printed instructions and a printed list of topic-related items. Periodically, include printed reminders for the learner to check her bingo sheet. Obviously, the learner is not competing with anyone else; instead, she is using the bingo sheet to alert her brain to look for certain concepts.

Here is an example of printed instructions:

* *After reading these instructions, take a blank piece of paper and fold it into eight squares. From the list below, choose eight topic-related items that you want to know more about. Write these items, one per square, on your bingo sheet. Refer to your bingo paper as you work through this course. When you see an item covered, cross it out on your bingo sheet. When you have all items crossed out, write "Bingo!" across your paper in big letters. This activity will help your brain find and remember specific information.*

Here are examples of printed instructions during an online course:

▶ *Check your bingo sheet and cross out any items that have been covered in this course so far.*

▶ *Have you checked your bingo paper for items that have been covered? Cross them out.*

▶ *Remember to check your bingo paper and cross out the items you've already learned about.*

▶ *Refer to your bingo paper now and cross out the items that were part of the information covered in this section (chapter).*

▶ *Do you have all your bingo items crossed out? If not, go back through the course to find the ones you've missed. Read those sections again then cross out the remaining bingo items on your paper. Write "BINGO!" across the paper. Congratulations!*

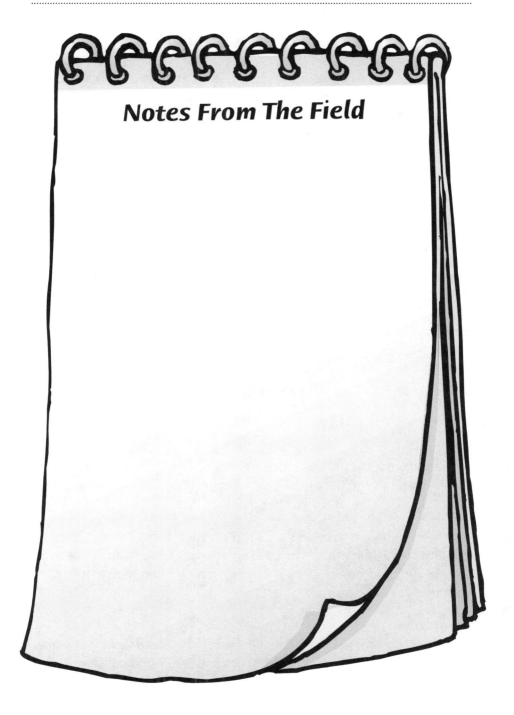

Notes From The Field

4. Fill-In-The-Blanks

While this is an often-used activity, and one that can easily be over-used, it is still worthwhile when introducing important concepts. It is also a good review exercise. Furthermore, with a little modification, it can become self-correcting, that is, learners are able to correct their own or each other's papers without your help. Make sure that there are enough words in the sentences to give the learners contextual clues.

Here is an example of a sentence with no contextual clues:

► _____ *and* _____ *are important for* _____.

Here is an example of a sentence with contextual clues:

► *Learners remember more when they* _____ *and* _____ *than when they just sit and listen.*

Duration: From one to five minutes.

Detailed Instructions:
Before the training, create a worksheet in which important words are missing from a list of bulleted sentences or concepts. Use underlined blank spaces where the missing words should be. Each learner should have his own copy of the worksheet.

During the content delivery, pause to give learners time to fill in the missing words as you cover the specific material. You might even have each phrase or sentence printed on a slide, first with blanks then with the words filled in.

Variations:
Self-Correcting Worksheet. Create the *Fill-In-The-Blanks* worksheet but with three modifications. First, print the answers, out of order, at

the bottom of the page. Second, make sure that the answers fit into the blanks in just one way so that all the answers make sense only if the filled-in answers are correct. Third, print the handout instructions at the top of the page as follows:

▶ *For each numbered sentence, choose the correct phrase from the list below and write it on the lines. <u>You can use each phrase only once and each sentence must make sense when you read it aloud.</u> You can work by yourself or with others in your table group.*

Give learners time to work individually or collaboratively to fill in the blanks and perform the self-corrections. If time allows, follow this with a short, whole-group discussion about the content of the worksheet. Answer any questions learners might still have.

Pre/Post Fill-Ins. Use the worksheet as a pre/post activity. At the beginning of the class, have learners take a minute or so to guess what might go in the blanks. They can work individually or collaboratively and write their guesses in the margins. Doing this will cause them to think about what they already know and alert them to what will be coming up in the content delivery. This variation also changes the way in which they pay attention to the content because now they want to know if their guesses are right or wrong. Finally, it enables them to use contextual clues that are content-related. Essentially, they cover the content on the worksheet three times: once as a pre-activity; once during the content deliver; once as a post-activity.

Flashcard Fill-Ins. Same exercise; different medium. Instead of using a worksheet, print one phrase/sentence (with important words left out, of course) per index card. Duplicate the cards and place one card set on each table. Tell the groups to lay out their card sets so that the group members can read them.

During the content delivery, pause at various times for groups to collaboratively select the card that goes with the content you are covering. Have them fill in their anwers and check their answers with other table groups or with you. Then you continue with the next content segment.

You can change this variation by adding an answer key to each card set. Groups work collaboratively on the cards then check their answers against the answer key.

For eLearning;

This activity is an easy one to include in self-study courses since it works so well with printed material. The *Pre/Post Fill-In* variation is also excellent for elearning.

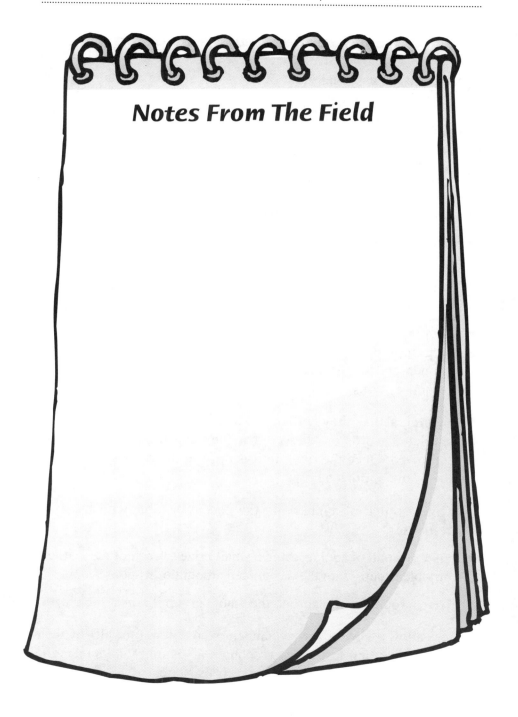

Notes From The Field

5. Beat-The-Clock (written version)

This activity is essentially the same as the moving and talking versions, but learners write their responses instead.

Duration: One or two minutes.

Detailed Instructions:
You can structure this activity four ways:

▶ Learners work individually, competing against time and each other.

▶ Learners work collaboratively in small groups, competing against time and the other groups.

▶ Learners work collaboratively as one group, competing against the clock.

▶ Give a specific number of designated responses that learners or groups need to attain in order to beat the clock. Or leave it open-ended: the individual or group with the most correct responses wins.

Tell learners that they will have one minute to write as many topic-related words or phrases that they can think of during the time allowed. Once the time limit is up, end the activity with your choice of the options below:

▶ Give a round of applause to the person or table with the most responses.

▶ Give a round of applause and a small prize to each of the learners or table groups with the designated amount of responses.

▶ Give a round of applause to the whole group if it beat the clock.

If time allows, have a few volunteers read a few (not all) of their responses. Reading just a few responses gives other volunteers the opportunity to read responses from their lists, too.

Variations:

See the activities titled *Graffiti Time* and *Stick 'Em Up* on pages 210-211. Have the learners use words and phrases instead of images.

For eLearning:

For a synchronous class, the instructions are the same as if the class were face-to-face. For an asynchronous course, examples of printed instructions are:

▶ *After reading this, give yourself one minute to write as many topic-related facts as you can remember, without going back through the material. At the end of one minute, stop writing and check your facts against the material in this section (chapter). How many facts did you remember correctly? Write the number here.*

▶ *Now take one minute to write as many facts about this topic as you can. See if you can write at least ten facts in the sixty seconds. Stop when the time is up and check your answers. Then continue reading.*

▶ *What do you remember? Time yourself as you write as many facts as you can in one minute. Then check your facts and continue reading.*

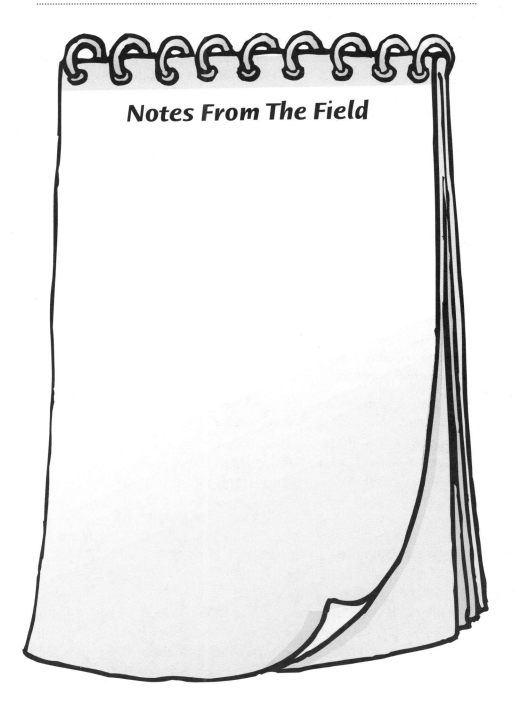

Notes From The Field

Working The Principle: Shorter Trumps Longer

The basic concept that underlies all exercises in this section is: *the brain remembers shorter content pieces better than longer ones.*

Listed below are five strategies to help you apply *Shorter Trumps Longer* to your own instruction:

▶ **Time Your Talk.** Before the training, time your segments of instruction to make sure they last no longer than ten minutes each (up to twenty minutes will still work; learning diminishes after that). While delivering the material, be aware of how long you are talking. Use a timer, a printed reminder, or a volunteer to help you stay within the time limit. Remember, the review activities between lecture segments need only be a minute or two. Then continue delivering the content from where you left off.

▶ **Space Your Slides.** Rather than showing a series of slides, consider showing one or two slides that capture the essence of a concept. Present the rest of the material using a different method, such as a story, case study, handout, or wall chart. In other words, make the slides the exception rather than the rule. Be sure to blank out the screen during the non-slide segments. Use a blank slide or press the Shift-B keys for this.

▶ **Check In With Learners.** If you're not sure how long you've been lecturing, or if you're not sure how much longer learners can listen effectively, ask them. Have them give you a signal (thumbs up for yes, thumbs down for no) as to whether or not they can listen longer, need to do a quick review activity, or need a break.

▶ **Bracket The Content**. Sometimes you can string two or three ten-minute content segments together if you bracket them with memorable openings and closings. An example is to begin a segment with a story, then complete the story at the end of the lecture. Another example is to begin with a question and accept all answers without stating which answers are correct. At the end of the content segment, see if any learners have changed their responses. Then share the answers you had in mind.

▶ **Need-To-Know Versus Nice-To-Know**. Perhaps the most challenging thing you will ever do in your teaching/training career will be to take a long, hard look at the content you cover and make the difficult decision to separate the need-to-know from the nice-to-know material. *Then teach only the need-to-know concepts.*

This means that you ask yourself, "What is it that my learners need to know, the lack of which would adversely affect their jobs?" Or, "What would happen if my students don't remember this?"

In all probability, much of the content you cover are details that support the major concepts; details that are nice, but not necessary. Only you can be the judge of that.

I'm not suggesting that you leave out those details. Just put them after the important concepts and include them only if you have the time. Or put the nice-to-know material in a handout, on a resource list, on a wall chart, or on an Intranet site. Only the need-to-know content should be on slides.

For elearning, cutting out the nice-to-know content is critical for maintaining learner interest and controlling the length of the course. If content qualifies as nice-to-know, create an optional branch or link to it. In addition, put content in a downloadable, printable format to enable learners to access and print it later.

Activities That
Put The Principle To Work

This principle is different from the other five because it is an integral part of each activity described in this book. All the activities apply *Shorter Trumps Longer*. Most of the exercises take from one to five minutes to do. A few take up to ten minutes. That's it. You'll have time to use them while teaching the need-to-know content.

Since all activities in Part Four are based on *Shorter Trumps Longer*, you can choose from any of them to put this principle to work. Flip through the pages and flag the activities that appeal to you. Of course, write your field notes on the pages so that you can make these activities work even better in the future.

Working The Principle:
Different Trumps Same

For this principle, think about the elements of your class that are always the same. Then change some of them.

More specifically, pay attention to the learning environment, the media and the materials you use, how you begin and end the class, and how you structure the content delivery and learning activities—in other words, your teaching routine.

Here are five strategies to help you apply this principle:

They're Not In School Anymore. Most people in the United States have spent twelve years or more in classrooms. If the environment you teach in looks like a traditional classroom, it will, in all probability, trigger learner boredom and perhaps anxiety. So do the opposite: change the environment so that it does *not* look like school. Arrange desks, chairs, or tables so that learners can sit in small groups. Hang colorful, content-related charts on walls. Have a variety of *Mark-Up* materials arranged on the tables. Have breakout areas that learners can use for paired or small-group discussions: chairs arranged in circles, empty spaces for standing groups, bean bags or cushions for floor-sitting. Make the environment look *different* from traditional classrooms.

Surprise Them. Use a different opening or closing activity from what you usually do, especially if your company has a standardized course structure, the class is multi-day, or you've had the students in a previous class. Change the pace of the instruction: fast, slow, rapid-fire questions, quiet time for reflection, a touching story mixed in with facts and figures. Tell learners to stand for one activity, sit for another, move around the room for a third. Keep them wondering what will come next.

Mix Them Up. Change the members of the groups. Even if they sit in the same table groups, make sure they have opportunities to work with others in the room. Have them form random standing pairs, tri-ads, or small groups with learners from other tables. If the class lasts more than half a day, tell learners to switch tables and groups for the second half of the day. Or have them switch seating each time the class meets.

Something Old, Something New. Combine the routine with the novel. The activity *Dot-Voting* on page 241 is a good example of this. Stating the learning outcomes (objectives) at the beginning of train-ing is routine; using an activity with movement, charts, and colored dots is a novel way to do it.

It's For You, Too. Changing your instructional routine is as impor-tant for you as it is for your learners. Your brain thrives on change, whether or not you consciously know it. When you change the ele-ments of content delivery and the learning environment, you increase your own enthusiasm, energy, and passion for teaching.

My Notes

Five Activities That
Put The Principle To Work

The next five activities primarily use *Different Trumps Same.* As with previous activities, many of these also combine this principle with others.

Flag the activities you decide to use, then write your field notes so that you can make them work even better in the future.

1. Dot-Voting

This is an excellent opening activity in which you use traditional learning outcomes (or learning objectives, as many instructors call them) in a very non-traditional way.

Learners have little reason to pay close attention when the instructor creates, prints, and/or presents the learning objectives. However, with *Dot-Voting,* learners are actively involved in reading, evaluating, prioritizing, paying attention to, and remembering the learning outcomes of the training.

This activity also brackets the learning because it is both an opening and closing exercise. For example, learners do *Dot-Voting* at the beginning of a training session. Then, at the end, they discuss the most significant concepts they learned that pertain to the outcomes they had originally dotted.

Duration: From one to five minutes.

Detailed Instructions:
Before the class or training, post the learning outcomes on a wall chart. Make sure you use dark-colored markers and print in large letters so that the words are easy to read from across the room. Leave enough space after or under each outcome for the dots. Also make sure that each table group has a sheet of large, colored dots (available at most office supply stores).

At the beginning of the training, explain that the learning outcomes are printed on the wall chart. Tell the learners to stand and place a dot beside (after, under) the one outcome that is most important *to him or her.* Once everyone has done this, they all return to their seats. If time allows, have them share with their table group which outcome they dotted and why.

After the *Dot-Voting* is finished, point out to the group which outcomes have the most dots and the significance of that in terms of the group's interests. This is important for three reasons: it will focus learners on the outcomes once more; it will show learners that you are paying attention to where their interests lie; and it will illustrate what the majority of learners are most interested in. Explain that you will still address all learning outcomes; you may just spend more time on the outcomes in which the group is most interested.

During your content delivery, refer to the *Dot-Voting* wall chart whenever appropriate. Use the wall chart at the end of the training to review what was covered. Give learners time to compare and contrast what they knew at the beginning of the class with what they know at the end. Have them share the information they learned that pertained to the specific learning outcomes they dotted.

Variations:

Paper Outcomes. Print the list of learning outcomes on a handout and pass out copies to the learners. They do the same with this list that they do with the wall chart: read the list, evaluate it in terms of what is important to *them,* and then place a colored dot beside the one or two outcomes that are their top priority.

Personal Goal. In addition to doing the *Paper Outcomes* variation, tell learners to also write a personal learning goal on a Post-It® note and place it on the outcomes page. One of the closing activities at the end of class will then be to come back to this page for a paired or table group discussion about what each person learned that was connected to his personal goal.

Card-Set Outcomes. The basic activity remains the same; you are just changing the medium. Instead of listing the learning outcomes on a wall chart or handout, make a set of cards, one set per table group. On each card, print one learning outcome in a large bold letters so learners can read the cards from a standing position. Each group stands (to add movement to the activity) and spreads out the cards on the table so that everyone in the group can read them. They all read the cards and then discuss the outcomes in terms of what *the group* considers the most important. The group places colored dots on the cards they have decided are the most important outcomes.

Another variation is to have group members do the *Card-Set Outcomes* activity individually. Once they spread out the cards on the table, each group member reads them all and then dots the one or two outcomes that are top priority for him or her.

For eLearning:

Do the *Paper Outcomes* variation for the learner to download and print before continuing the course. Examples of written instructions on the page are:

▶ *The learning outcomes for this course are listed below. Place a colored dot (or draw one) in front of the outcomes that are the most important to <u>you</u>. You will come back to this page at the end of the course to review what you learned.*

▶ *Place a colored dot beside the two learning outcomes you think will help you the most in your work (on the job, in achieving your goals, in passing this course, in your life).*

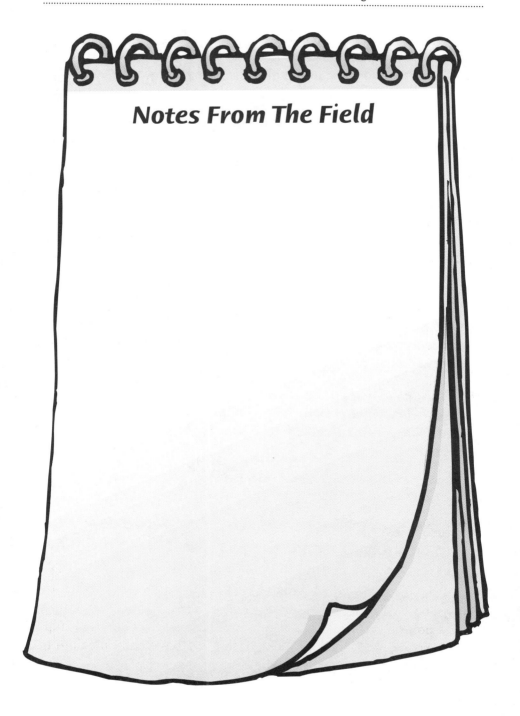

Notes From The Field

2. Sculpt It

With this activity, learners use three-dimensional materials to represent topic-related facts, concepts, main ideas, procedures, and the like. The three-dimensional representations are actually visual metaphors for important content.

Use this activity in place of, or in addition to, traditional note-taking. You might also use it as a closing activity to review content in a way quite different from the usual summary exercises.

In addition, the sculptures become "souvenirs" of the learning journey—visual and tactile reminders of important content—when learners take them home and display them on a desktop, counter, shelf, bulletin board, or wall.

Here is a list of many of the materials that work well for *Sculpt It:* pipe cleaners, PlayDoh®, Model Magic® (another clay-type medium), Legos®, foam shapes and letters, cardboard, small sticks such as tongue depressors, straws, and colored paper (all sizes and shapes). You can find most of the suggested materials in craft, hobby, toy, and discount stores.

Depending upon the medium you choose, you will also need glue or tape, scissors, and writing materials (colored markers, crayons, or colored pens) for each table group.

Duration: From one to ten minutes.

Detailed Instructions:
For the basic *Sculpt It,* choose one type of material (example: pipe cleaners). Place a selection of multi-colored pipe cleaners at each table. It doesn't matter if learners tinker with them during the training. At the point when you want learners to create their own 3-D sculptures, explain to them that they will be using a different medium to represent a major concept from the content covered.

Learners work collaboratively with their table group to choose a top-ic-related concept and to create one pipe cleaner sculpture. You set the time limit for the activity. In one or two minutes they will create simple sculptures; allow up to five minutes and the sculptures will be more complex.

At the end of the time limit, ask volunteers to hold up their group's sculpture and explain what concept it represents. If the sculpture is complex, volunteers share the details of the representation (example: *"This part of the sculpture stands for… this part here represents…"*). End each group's presentation with a round of applause.

If possible, display all the sculptures on a separate table where the whole class can see them. Allow table groups or a volunteer from each table group to take them back to their workplace at the end of class.

Variations:
Make It Personal. Learners create their own sculptures. They explain their sculptures to their table group and take the sculptures home as souvenirs of the training and as a reminder of what they learned.

3-D Table. Designate one table in the room as the *Sculpt It* table. Place all the craft items on this table. Learners have a choice of doing the activity collaboratively with their table groups or individually. They have to go to the *Sculpt It* table to get the materials they need, then take their craft items back to their table. There are three advantages to putting all *Sculpt It* materials in one place versus scattered among all tables. First, you don't have to purchase as many items; a few of each variety will do as groups won't all choose the same item. Second, the craft items will be less distracting during the content delivery. Third, there will be more movement as learners walk back and forth to obtain materials.

The two main disadvantages to this variation are space and time. You will need more space around the *Sculpt It* table to make the materials more accessible. You will also need to lengthen the activity time so the learners can choose their materials.

Chart Collages. This variation is probably best when pairs, triads, or small groups work collaboratively on a wall chart. Using glue or tape, they stick the craft materials to the chart paper. Often, the pieces become part of a larger visual metaphor for concepts learned. If you wish, tell learners to label the collage pieces and print a title on the chart. At the end of the activity, groups explain their collages to the whole group. You can then hang all the charts on walls to form a gallery of sorts.

For eLearning:

I know an elearning instructor who, because he teaches synchronous classes, sends out a small box of craft items to each learner a week before the class begins. He also instructs them to think about how they might use these materials to represent the topic. Learners bring their boxes to the class. The instructor uses the *Make It Personal* variation above. Learners take digital photos of their finished sculptures and upload the photos to an electronic bulletin board which is shared by all.

Here is another suggestion for synchronous classes where two or more learners are attending in the same physical space, such as an office. Before the class begins, provide a printed list of possible office-type materials for them to have available: colored markers, colored paper, tape, scissors, Post-It® notes (similar to the *Mark-Up* materials). Follow the *Sculpt It* instructions or the *Make It Personal* variation above.

For asynchronous classes, use the *Say It With Symbols* instructions on page 196 instead.

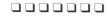

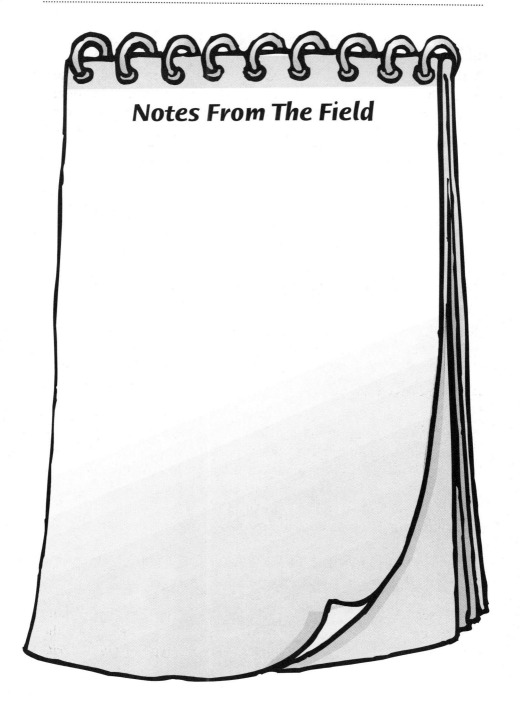

Notes From The Field

3. Learner's Toolbox

With this activity, learners use real boxes as holders for notes they take. What makes this note-taking activity different from a traditional pencil/paper worksheet is that learners actually fill these "toolboxes" with index card or Post-It® note *Quick Writes:* ideas, concepts, facts, summary statements, action plans, and so forth.

You can find small boxes for economical prices at most craft stores. If you purchase white or non-glossy boxes, learners can write on the boxes as well. Most learners enjoy the novelty of this kind of note-taking activity.

Add colored markers, dots, stickers, and foam letters to the mix and the toolboxes become colorful reminders of the course content.

Duration: Five minutes to decorate the toolboxes; one minute for each *Quick Write* that learners do and place inside their boxes.

Detailed Instructions:

Before class, purchase enough small boxes so that each learner has one. Put the boxes out on the tables, along with the other materials learners can use to decorate their boxes. Make sure there are enough index cards and Post-It® notes available for each group, as well as colorful writing materials.

During the beginning of the class, give learners from three to five minutes to decorate their boxes. Instruct them to print their name on the box as well as one personal learning goal for the class.

At different times during the class, stop and tell learners to do a *Quick Write* (see page 221 for ideas). Learners do these short, one-minute writing exercises on index cards or Post-It® notes, then place the cards or notes inside their toolboxes. Vary the type of *Quick Write* activity each time.

At the end of the class, learners do one or more closing activities with the boxes. Examples:

▶ While upbeat music plays, learners pass their box to other learners who write encouraging remarks *("Nice to have met you ... Keep on shining ... Good luck in all you do ...")* and then sign them.

▶ Learners form standing groups and share one or two of the best ideas from their toolbox collections.

▶ Learners write themselves encouraging remarks on their own toolbox. Or they write their action plan: *what* they plan to do with what they learned, *when* they plan to do it, and *who* they will tell they did it. They can also put a future date on the box which indicates when they will open the box and see how much they remember.

▶ Learners collect a few email addresses from others with whom they want to stay in contact and write these on the sides of their box. If privacy is an issue, they can write the email addresses on index cards and put them inside the box.

Variations:

Learner's Toolbag. Instead of using boxes, use small blank, paper lunch bags. You can find white or multi-colored ones at most craft or stationery supply stores. Most grocery stores carry the standard brown ones. Or, for online bulk purchases, do an Internet search for "blank white paper lunch bags."

Origami Containers. Learners can also make their own origami boxes or any kind of paper container. Do an Internet search for "origami containers" to see what is there. The upside of this variation is that you can sometimes match the container to a topic-related theme and most learners enjoy the origami aspect. The downside is the time it takes to create the containers. You have to add about five extra minutes to the activity time.

For eLearning:

Have a downloadable, printable handout with a large picture of a box or bag available for learners. You can either draw/scan it, or create it using free clip art. Examples of the printed instructions are:

▶ *This is your toolbox. During this course, print the most important facts, ideas you have, and anything you want to remember on this box. Use colored pens or markers to color-code, if you like. After you have finished the course, tape the box on your bulletin board or near your computer. The toolbox will remind you of what you have learned and will help you remember what you thought was important.*

▶ *In this toolbox, you will write important facts, main ideas, and anything you want to remember. Write them as you work through the content. In effect, this is your summary page of the information that's most important to you.*

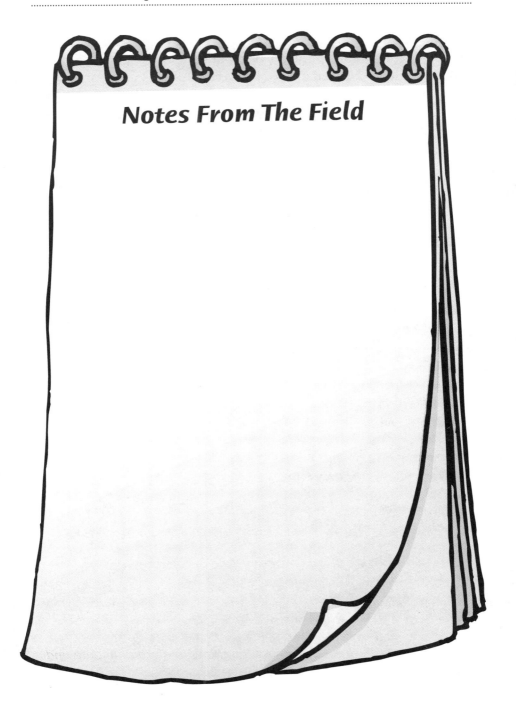

Notes From The Field

4. Looks Like, Sounds Like

This activity uses motions and sounds to represent main ideas, major concepts, or emotions (for example, how learners feel about what they have learned). In essence, the exercise is a summarization method without using traditional verbal or written summary statements.

This activity is especially useful as part of the closing or whenever you or the learners need a novel, energizing way of wrapping up a content segment.

Duration: From two to five minutes, depending upon the size of the group.

Detailed Instructions:
You specify what will be represented: main ideas, major concepts, or how learners are feeling about what they've learned so far. You also specify how table groups will represent this: with a motion, a sound, or both.

Table group members work together to create their motion and/or sound. Give them about one minute to do this. At the end of the time limit, each group stands and presents its motion/sound in front of the class. Groups applaud each other.

Variations:
Personally Yours. Learners work individually, each creating a motion/sound. They share their creations with their table groups.

Tell It, Don't Do It. As a verbal metaphor, learners or groups simply tell each other or the whole group what the motion and sound might be that represent their feelings about the topic or the topic as a whole. Some examples are:

▶ *We would represent this sales training with a group huddle and a shout of "Go, team, go!"*

▶ *This data entry procedure looks like jumping jacks because the sequenced, repetitive motion represents the procedural steps that have to be done in order. It sounds like a train that starts off slowly and gets faster and faster, kind of like the data entry employee who builds up speed as he becomes more experienced with the procedure.*

▶ *This customer service training looks like two people shaking hands, signifying the relationship between customer and employee. It sounds like "Ahhhhhh," showing how satisfying this relationship can be.*

▶ *We think this financial planning class could be represented with a person standing with arms outstretched and palms up as if receiving abundance from everywhere. The sound could be the opening bell of the stock market.*

For eLearning: For synchronous classes, use the *Tell It, Don't Do It* variation. For asynchronous courses, do the *Say It With Symbols* activity on page 196 instead.

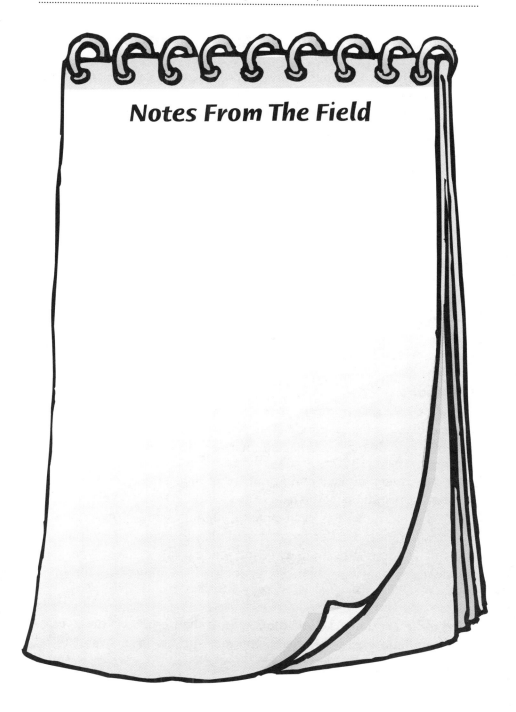

Notes From The Field

5. Rhythm, Rap, And Rhyme

This activity incorporates the wonderfully memorable elements of songs, poems, rap, advertising jingles, and any rhythmical language that seems to stick forever inside the human brain because of the rhythm, rhyme, and repetition. This exercise is certainly a novel one: full of contrast, emotion, and meaning. It generates a lot of creativity and enthusiasm among the learners.

Duration: From five to ten minutes, depending upon the size of the group.

Detailed Instructions:
As a closing activity, tell learners they will have about three minutes to create a group poem, song, or rap that summarizes what they've learned or the main ideas of the class. At the end of the time limit, they share their verbal creations with the whole group. End each group's presentation with a rousing round of applause.

Variations:
Slogan Or Theme Song. Learners follow the same instructions, but instead of a poem, song, or rap, they create a one-line slogan or the title of a new theme song that summarizes the class content.

Post The Poem. Have small groups print their poems, songs, or rap on chart paper and post the papers around the room. The class stands in front of each chart as each small group takes a turn presenting its poem, song, or rap. After the first reading, the whole group applauds the small group. If desired, a second reading takes place, where the whole group reads the poem, song, or rap aloud, along with the small group.

Electronic Versions. Tell learners to post their creations on an electronic bulletin board, blog site, Intranet site, or in an email to all participants.

For eLearning:

For synchronous training, have learners create their poems, songs, or rap in text-based chat rooms. For an asynchronous training, do the *Slogan Or Theme Song* variation instead. Examples of printed instructions are:

▶ *Think about the content of this class. If you were an advertising company that had to create a one-line slogan to capture the essence of this content, what would the slogan be? Write it here.*

▶ *Make up a title to a new theme song that represents the main idea of this course. Write the title here.*

▶ *Think about what you've learned. Write either a one-line slogan or the title for a theme song that represents one or more of the major concepts. Write your slogan or theme song title here.*

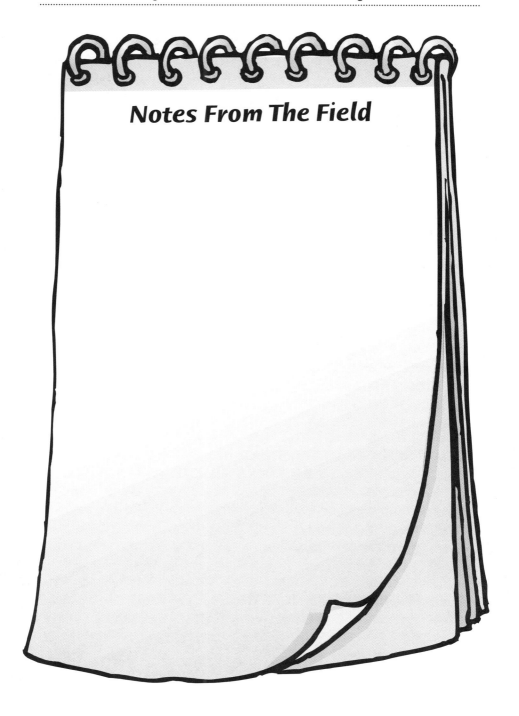

Notes From The Field

Where To Go From Here

The way I see it:
If you need both of your hands
for whatever it is you're doing,
then your brain should probably be in on it too.
Ellen DeGeneres

The next steps are up to you. To continue your own learning journey, you have a number of options to choose from:

▶ *Use* this book as a resource for strategies and activities whenever you design and facilitate a learning experience.

▶ *Teach* what you've learned. You will master the material and help others become better at what they do.

▶ From now on, *keep* the six learning principles in mind whenever you see, read about, or use other instructional methods and learning activities. Ask yourself if they apply any of the principles. If yes, which principles do they use? If they don't, then consider discarding them in favor of methods and activities that *do* apply one or more of the principles.

▶ *Design* your own instructional strategies and learner activities based on the six learning principles in this book.

▶ *Post* the principles where you can see them as you teach.

▶ *Explore* the resources in Part Five to deepen your own understanding of the brain science behind effective teaching and learning.

▶ *Keep* the learners in mind every step of the way.

▶ It always bears repeating: *"Take* what you can use and let the rest go by" (with thanks to author Ken Kesey).

▶ *Do* what you love; *love* what you do. All else is a game of cards.

This book is the brainchild of my brainchild.
It is my brain-grandchild.
– paraphrased from Michael Scott

❏ ❏ ❏ ❏ ❏ ❏ ❏

PART FIVE

Brain Science Resources

Using The Resources

*New research into cognitive functioning—
how the brain works—
proves that bullet points are the least effective way
to deliver important information.
Neuroscientists are finding that
what passes as a typical presentation
is usually the worst way to engage your audience.*

Carmine Gallo

Throughout this book, I've used the term *brain science* as a synonym for *cognitive neuroscience* or *cognitive science,* that is, how the human brain takes in, stores, retrieves, and uses information. As I pointed out in *Training from the BACK of the Room* (2009), the brain is being studied by many people in various fields: scientists, physicians, biologists, chemists, psychologists, educators, trainers, philosophers, anthropologists, and technologists, to name a just a few. Author Patricia Wolfe said it best: "The more we understand the brain, the better we're able to design instruction to match how the brain learns best" (2001, p. 2). This book has been my attempt to help you apply some of the extensive research to your own instruction.

Part Five will further your understanding of brain science. The resources I've included here are by no means complete. I have chosen information, books, and websites that have been meaningful to me and that I believe will be meaningful to you. Of course, as with all learning, I expect you to pick and choose: some resources will appeal to you and others won't. I believe there is enough diversity here for most readers to find something of interest.

Here is an overview of what Part Five includes:

The Six Trumps® Workshop. This is the facilitator's guide for a forty-five minute introductory workshop. Two college faculty members assisted in the creation of this guide so that other educators and trainers could use it to introduce the six trumps to their respective audiences.

Branching Stories: The Tale Behind *Choose Your Own Learning*. This section contains the history of how Part Two in this book came to be and the resources that were useful in its creation. It also includes more information about branching stories as a learning method.

The Biologist And The Educator. Two authors deserve special praise for the application of brain science to teaching and learning. This section includes more information about them and the books they've written.

Brain Science Books. In this section, I've listed the resources that form the foundation for *Using Brain Science To Make Training Stick*. I've also included some other, relevant resources. I added personal comments about each book. Some books I highly recommend; others are for readers interested in more specialized material.

More Book Resources. These are books about teaching and training, although not necessarily about brain science. I consider most of them practical resources to help enhance the effectiveness of instruction. I've included comments about each.

Brain Science Websites. There are thousands of relevant websites that contain news clips, articles, products, and other information about the human brain and how it learns. These are a few of the websites that I have found useful.

Sharon's Books, Website, And Bio. For readers interested in the books I have written, free articles from my website, and a bit of information about me, look here.

We should not be too fastidious
about where great ideas come from.
Ultimately, they all come from
a wrinkled organ that at its healthiest
has the color and consistency of toothpaste.

Alice W. Flaherty

The Six Trumps® Workshop

During the two years prior to this book's publication, I researched and field-tested the book's material with many audiences: corporate trainers, school district and college educators, medical professionals, motorcycle safety instructors, law enforcement professionals, and learning specialists from nonprofit agencies.

The following facilitator's guide is for a forty-five minute workshop that introduces the six learning principles. I am deeply grateful to Beverly Woolery, director of the Educator Preparation Institute at Polk State College in Winter Haven, Florida, and Rebecca Pugh, a college education professor there, for their contributions to this guide.

The guide will give you an engaging, interactive way to introduce the six learning principles to your audiences. The principles are the same whether you teach educational classes or corporate training. If you want your audiences to know about the principles, the guide is an excellent resource. It contains the script (printed in italics), materials list, instructions, and sources for the handout materials and slide set. As always, it is up to you to modify the guide to suit your instructional needs and the learning needs of your audiences.

Materials Needed

This facilitator's guide.

One deck of standard playing cards per small table group.

▶ Facilitator card deck.

▶ A wristwatch with a sweep (second) hand, or some other type of one-minute timer.

▶ One postcard for each participant. This is the handout. To find the free postcard master copy, log onto my website, *www. Bowperson.com*, click the *Articles* link, and scroll down to find *The Six Trumps® Workshop Postcard*. It is PDF-formatted and is downloadable with Adobe Acrobat (get the free Adobe Acrobat Reader at *www.adobe.com*).

▶ Six learning principle cards, one card per table. You may have to print more than one set if you have more than six tables. Or you may have to put more cards than one on each table if you have fewer tables. *The Six Trumps® Workshop Table Cards* are also located in the *Articles* section of my website.

▶ Facilitator slide set. *The Six Trumps® Workshop Slide Set* is also in the *Articles* section.

▶ Pen/pencil for each participant.

▶ Facilitator noisemaker (whistle, chimes, music, or other auditory signaling device).

▶ Audio-visual equipment: LCD projector, screen, computer or USB flash drive containing the slide set, appropriate electrical cords, microphone (if necessary).

Room Set-Up

▶ Table rounds of 4 - 6 participants per table. If there are individual desks, cluster the desks into groups of four. If there are rectangular tables, cluster the chairs around them instead of lining up the chairs on one side of the tables.

▶ Screen, whiteboard or blank area in front of the room on which to project the slides. Be sure all participants can see the screen.

▶ Enough room around the furniture to allow for participant movement while working in standing groups.

Instructions And Script

Introduction. Slide #1.

Hold up a deck of cards and say:

When you play most card games, there is one suit in the deck, or one card in the suit, that beats all the others. The trump card or suit is the best one to have. "To trump" means to use the best card or best suit to win the hand or card game.

In this session, a card game is a metaphor for learning and the trump cards represent ways of learning that work <u>for the learners</u>. These learning methods are based on "cognitive neuroscience," that is, the brain science about how humans learn. These brain-based learning methods "trump" more traditional ways of learning.

During this workshop, you will actively explore six learning principles that come from current brain science. You will use the principles even as you are learning about them.

Activity: Standing Survey.
Tell participants to designate a card dealer for their table. The dealer is the person who has played more types of card games than the other group members. Give them a minute to find out who that person is.

Direct the dealers to shuffle the cards and give one card to each group member. Once each participant has a card, tell them to stand and find someone from another table who has the same suit: clubs, diamonds, hearts, or spades. They form standing pairs or triads (tell them to make sure no one is left out).

Say: *You just increased your ability to learn by about 15% - 20%. Why? Because you stood up and <u>moved</u>. Movement increases the amount of oxygen delivered to the brain. Oxygen enhances cognitive function. Yet, in most classes, the learners sit while the instructor moves. In a brain-based class, learners have opportunities to stand and move.*

Quickly introduce yourself to your partner(s) and share one fact you already know about, or have heard or read about, how the brain learns. The person with the highest numbered card goes first. Then each participant takes a turn in descending order of card numbers. You have about two minutes to do this. When you hear this signal (use your noisemaker), *thank your partner(s), remain standing, and turn your attention back to me.*

Signal the end of the activity. Participants do not return to their seats yet. They stand and listen for the next set of instructions.

Activity: Beat-The-Clock (talking version).

Say: *To collect some of the facts about human learning that you discussed with your standing partner(s), we are going to do a quick "Beat-The-Clock" shout out. As a group, we need at least fifteen facts in sixty seconds. When I say "Go!" take turns shouting out a fact that was mentioned in your discussions. I will time you and count the facts.* Start the activity and encourage them to shout out facts. Accept all facts. End the activity when one minute is up. Have them give themselves a round of applause. Then say: *In addition to what you already know, let's add the six learning principles to the mix.*

Activity: Data Hunt.

Say: *You are going on a Data Hunt to gather the six learning principles. For this activity, you will need your postcard and a pen/pencil* (hold up a card for them to see). *These items are located where you were sitting. You will be filling in the blanks on the front of the card. The information you need is in the room. Look around, find the information, and fill in your card. When you have all six learning principles filled in, return to your seat. Sitting down is your signal that you have finished the activity.*

Allow about three minutes for them to complete the Data Hunt. Then signal the end of the activity and direct the participants who are still standing to sit down.

Activity: **Turn And Talk**. Slide #2.

Say: *Brain research tells us that, if we are exposed to information six times <u>and</u> in six different ways, we will usually remember the information a lot longer than if we just hear it once or read it once. In doing the Data Hunt, you were exposed to the learning principles three times: first, by hunting for the printed information; second, by reading the printed information; third, by writing it down on your postcards.*

Now let's add a fourth and fifth exposure. We'll begin by reading all six principles aloud together. Point to the slide and have the participants read the principles aloud with you. Remind them that this will help them remember the information longer.

Say: *In addition to repeated exposure, you are using multi-sensory learning to help you remember the concepts: seeing, hearing, writing, saying, and moving.*

Content Delivery (lecture segment). Slides #3 - #8.
Explain that this is their fifth exposure to each of the six learning principles. As you show each slide, add one or two more facts about each principle that you feel are important for workshop participants to know. Use the facts from this book. You will have to decide for yourself what the most important facts are for each of the six learning principles. *Do not* print the facts on the slides, but rather lecture from index cards or your own notes. Make this lecture no longer than ten minutes in length, shorter if you can. Time it before facilitating the workshop so that you do not go over the ten-minute limit.

Activity: **Talking Cards (small group discussion)**. Slide #9.
Tell the card dealers to give each group member one more card (they should each have two cards now).

Say: *This is the sixth exposure to the learning principles. You are going to have five minutes to brainstorm ways you can put the principles to use in your own classes. But there is a catch.*

Each time someone speaks, that person lays down one card in the middle of the table. Once someone has put two cards in the middle of the table, he or she cannot speak again until everyone else has spoken. Ready? Go.

Signal the end of the five minutes. Tell the learners to write on the back of their postcards two or three ideas from the discussion that they can use in their own classes or training programs. Thank participants for sharing their ideas with their colleagues.

Activity: Trump Card Wins.

Tell the groups to give their card dealers a round of applause. Then direct the dealers to collect all playing cards, shuffle the deck, and turn over one card.

Say: *This is your table group's trump suit, meaning that whatever suit the card is—club, diamond, heart, or spade—that is the winning suit. Now the dealer will deal a card to each of you.* Wait until this is done. *Whoever has the highest card <u>in the trump suit</u> wins the deck of cards.* If no one has a trump suit card, direct the dealer to deal another round of cards. Also tell groups to applaud the winner of the deck.

Conclusion Activity: Turn And Talk. Slide #10.

Say: *Now it's test-time. This is your last exposure to the six learning principles. Each of you needs to cover your card and see if you can recite all six principles correctly to a partner. Then your partner does the same thing. If you both get them all, give yourselves a high-five. If you forget any principles, review the cards and recite them again.*

Give participants about a minute to do the activity. Use the signal to end the exercise, thank them for coming to the workshop, and have them give themselves a round of applause for their participation.

Branching Stories:
The Tale Behind *Choose Your Own Learning*

When I was an elementary school teacher in the early 1980s, I came across a series of children's books titled *Choose Your Own Adventure®*. At that time, the authors were R. A. Montgomery and Edward Packard. They called the series "gamebooks" and the books became immensely popular with kids all over the world. You can still find the entire original series, as well as dozens more, in bookstores and online at *www.amazon.com*.

The premise was brilliant in its simplicity: give kids choices while they read. Depending upon their choices, the stories change so that children can read the same book many times and have a totally different adventure each time.

In other words, the reader gets to decide what to do as the story unfolds, and the story changes according to the reader's decisions. Sounds a lot like computer games now, right? The media changed; the premise remained the same.

Around the same time I found the *Choose Your Own Adventure®* books, I was introduced to "programmed learning." This book-based system had three basic elements: it delivered information in small, printed bites; it was self-paced (the learner was in charge of how fast or slow she wanted to proceed); and it provided the learner with immediate feedback.

Programmed learning found its way into some educational materials and has since morphed into computerized instruction called the ILS approach (Integrated Learning Systems) used by many corporate training departments.

The book that best exemplifies programmed learning for adults is *Bobby Fisher Teaches Chess* (1982) by chess master Bobby Fisher (the book is still available on *www.amazon.com*). The book asks what you, the reader, would do in a certain chess situation. You choose an answer and then turn the page to see if you are correct or not. It gives you feedback as to why your answer is right or wrong. Sometimes it asks you to choose again, or it will give you another similar situation to solve. With this approach, you learn to play chess *by playing the game.*

During the 1990s and into the present decade, I experimented with simplified programmed learning models in the books I was writing. Then I read Clark Aldrich's *Learning by Doing* (2005) and found the chapter in his book about branching stories (pp. 7-17). In it, Aldrich describes computer-based models similar to *Choose Your Own Adventure®* and programmed learning. His models can be modified for text only, or used with a variety of media. For text-based learning (books, manuals, handouts, or online courses that are read-only), branching stories can take the form that I used in Part Two of this book. I described a real-life training situation and gave you a number of choices as responses. You turned to the page that contained your response and compared it with my answer there. Furthermore, even if you chose an incorrect response, you received feedback as to why it was not the correct one. In other words, *you learned as much from the wrong answers as you did from the right ones.* The point was to give you immediate feedback about any response you chose.

For multi-media instruction, branching stories can be both video and text-based. For example, a video segment shows a customer service scenario between a customer and a salesperson. Then the video stops and gives the learner three printed choices in the form of links. The learner clicks on one of the three links. It takes him to another video segment in which his choice is played out between the customer and salesperson. Then printed information tells him whether or not this was the best choice to make in this situation. If his selection is not the best choice, it gives him the link to the best choice so he can watch the "right" answer in action.

Aldrich describes a number of branching story variations. He includes models, applications with various media, examples, and factors that contribute (or not) to the success of the branching story. If you are intrigued by all of this, then consider using Aldrich's book as a resource.

In my opinion, branching stories hold unique and powerful possibilities for interactive learning, whether in classrooms, online, or self-study. My attempts to use this strategy in Part Two are pretty basic, but I'm already exploring how to write a training book that is a complex branching story in its entirety. Perhaps you, too, can see other uses for this unique learning model with the topics you teach.

As a final thought, do an Internet search for "branching stories." You'll find many websites offering articles and suggestions about other uses for this method of instruction.

The Biologist And The Educator

Many scholars have contributed to the field of brain science. Although there might be a few readers who will question the credibility of researchers whose degrees are in education or psychology rather than medicine or science, most will agree that their observations show a remarkable correlation to, and consistency with, the findings of the scientists.

Two such researchers deserve their own section in this book. One is a scientist; the other an educator. One approaches learning from the standpoint of the biology of the brain; the other from observing thousands of human beings in learning labs called classrooms. While I have quoted extensively from the biologist's research, the educator's work is every bit as important because it is the successful *application* of much of the brain science.

The molecular biologist I'm referring to is John Medina, author of *Brain Rules* (2008). If Medina's book had been published before I wrote *Training from the BACK of the Room*, I would have listed it in my top five favorites, and I would have used it as one of my primary sources, as I've done in this book. It has become my brain bible, so to speak, especially since Medina includes all sorts of possible ways to apply his research to our daily lives, whether at home, school, or work. Furthermore, Medina paints his research with stories that are full of novelty, contrast, emotion, relevancy, and meaning. It is at the top on my list of recommended reading. If you have a limited amount of time and can only read one brain science book, make it Medina's.

The educator (and now the director for Uncommon Schools) I'm referring to is Doug Lemov, author of *Teach Like a Champion* (2010). Lemov approached successful teaching and learning by first asking the question, "What is it that excellent teachers do that others can learn *how* to do?" From years of research and classroom observation, he put together a list of specific, concrete techniques that excellent teachers use, whether or not they are consciously aware of it.

Although written primarily for K-12 educators, many (not all) of the techniques on Lemov's list are applicable to adult education. Lemov's techniques aren't new; he simply describes them in terms that are easy to remember and use. He's given the techniques short, two-word titles to make them memorable and imbues them with his own unique brand of teaching. Some of the activity titles may sound familiar: Post It, Exit Tickets, Wait Time, Everybody Writes, Seat Signals, All Hands, Work the Clock, and Check for Understanding.

Most important are the learning results that occur in the classrooms where teachers apply Lemov's techniques. He cites "return on invest-ment," that is, numbers-based results showing increases in learning and retention levels when teachers consistently use these techniques with their students.

In my opinion, Lemov's list of techniques can be divided into two general categories: classroom management and learner engagement. Both are necessary for the success of adult learning as well as for kids in classrooms.

The distinctions between how children learn versus how adults learn are artificial. They were drawn about sixty years ago and based on erroneous assumptions. Back then our knowledge about how the human brain learned was very lim-ited. Cognitive neuroscience, as a field of study, was in its infancy.

Now we know more. Many instructors may not yet apply it, but at least the knowledge is there for the taking. Indeed, *application* is the next, most crucial step.

Lemov's book is exactly that: *applying* what we know about human learning in concrete, useful, effective, and easily identifiable ways. This is the reason why I've included Lemov's book as recommended reading and have given it a special description here.

Brain Science Books

Bowman, Sharon (2009). *Training From The BACK Of The Room*. San Francisco CA: Pfeiffer Company, a division of John Wiley & Sons. The sequel to *The Ten-Minute Trainer*. Includes sixty-five easy-to-use, learner-centered activities and the instructional design model I call the 4 Cs. Also includes much of the current brain research about human learning and a detailed chapter on Accelerated Learning. Highly recommended (of course!).

Bowman, Sharon (2005). *The Ten-Minute Trainer*. San Francisco CA: Pfeiffer Company, a division of John Wiley & Sons. A collection of 150 short, learner-centered activities that you can use with any topic and any group of learners. Also includes brain research not cited in *Training From The BACK Of The Room*. Highly recommended (I would buy it if it weren't already mine).

Caine, Renate; Cain, Geoffrey; McClintic, Carol; Klimek, Karl. (2005). *12 Brain/Mind Learning Principles In Action*. Thousand Oaks, CA: Corwin Press. A lengthy read geared primarily to educators, but with some good ideas for putting the brain science to use.

Cross, Jay. (2007). *Informal Learning*. San Francisco, CA: Pfeiffer Co. Definitely a paradigm-shifting kind of book, and a must-read if you want to understand where education, training, and learning is going in the twenty-first century. Highly recommended.

Gibb, Barry. (2007). *The Rough Guide To The Brain*. London, England: Rough Guides. A more physiological and medical approach to understanding the human brain, for those who want that slant.

Howard, Pierce. (2000). *The Owner's Manual For The Human Brain*. Marietta, GA: Bard Press. Information-packed with research primarily from the twentieth century. More theoretical than applicable.

Jensen, Eric. (2000). *Brain-Based Learning*. Thousand Oaks, CA: Corwin Press. Reader-friendly and filled with practical ways of applying the research to classroom instruction. Recommended.

Lemov, Doug. (2010). *Teach Like A Champion*. Although written for K-12 teachers, contains excellent strategies and techniques for those of us who teach adults. Highly recommended.

Medina, John. (2008). *Brain Rules.* Seattle, WA: Pear Press. The best of the best. What else can I say? Highly recommended. Buy it!

Meier, David. (2000). *The Accelerated Learning Handbook.* New York, NY: McGraw-Hill. The most comprehensive book ever written about Accelerated Learning, authored by the director of the Center for Accelerated Learning. Reader-friendly and highly practical—a must for every trainer and teacher. Highly recommended.

Ratey, John. (2002). *A User's Guide To The Human Brain.* New York, NY: Random House. An intense read and very psychiatric in its approach. More for the medically-minded, not the classroom instructor.

Sousa, David. (2006). *How The Brain Learns.* Thousand Oaks, CA: Corwin Press. A reader-friendly brain primer, covering most of the important neuroscientific research of the past decade. Recommended.

Sprenger, Marilee. (1999). *Learning And Memory: The Brain In Action.* Alexandria, VA: Association for Supervision and Curriculum Development (ASCD). An excellent resource for understanding how memory works. Recommended.

Stolovich, Harold; Keeps, Erica. (2002). *Telling Ain't Training.* Alexandria, VA: American Society for Training & Development (ASTD). Explains brain science in easy-to-digest bites, with lots of reader interaction to spice it up. Recommended.

Sylwester, Robert. (1995). *A Celebration Of Neurons: An Educator's Guide To The Human Brain.* Alexandria, VA: Association for Supervision and Curriculum and Development (ASCD). The educational application of cognitive neuroscience. A fine introduction to the field. Recommended.

Wolfe, Patricia. (2001). *Brain Matters.* Alexandria, VA: Association for Supervision and Curriculum Development (ASCD). Another excellent resource combining neuroscience with practical classroom application. Highly recommended.

More Book Resources

Aldrich, Clark. (2005). *Learning By Doing*. San Francisco, CA: Pfeiffer Co. A highly technical and detailed resource for designing computer-based training. Includes a comprehensive chapter on branching stories.

Allen, Michael. (2003). *Michael Allen's Guide To E-Learning*. Hoboken, NJ: John Wiley & Sons. Interesting perspectives on learning in general and elearning specifically. A must if you design computer-based training.

Backer, Lori; Deck, Michele. (2003). *The Presenter's EZ Graphics Kit*. Sterling, VA: Stylus Publishing. A beginner's step-by-step guide for creating interesting, visually-appealing graphics on charts, handouts, presentation software, and any printed material.

Barkley, Elizabeth; Cross, Patricia; Major, Howell. (2005). *Collaborative Learning Techniques*. San Francisco, CA: Jossey-Bass. A research-based book about cooperative and collaborative learning. Includes a collection of classroom-based strategies that are applicable to corporate training as well.

Bowman, Sharon. (2001). *Preventing Death By Lecture!* Glenbrook, NV: Bowperson Publishing. A short, easy read with dozens of quick activities—from one to five minutes in length—that you can use with any subject and any size group.

Bowman, Sharon. (1998). *How To Give It So They Get It!* Glenbrook, NV: Bowperson Publishing. For readers who want to explore the ways they learn, teach, train, and communicate. Includes detailed descriptions of the four major learning styles and easy-to-follow instructions for forty activities.

Bowman, Sharon. (1997). *Presenting With Pizzazz!* Glenbrook, NV: Bowperson Publishing. A training primer of tips and activities for learner engagement.

El-Shamy, Susan. (2004). *How To Design And Deliver Training For The New And Emerging Generations*. San Francisco, CA: Pfeiffer Co. Covers both research and practical application for teaching members of the generations following the baby boomers. Contains a wealth of easy ways to reach learners under the age of forty.

Heath, Chip and Dan. (2007). *Made To Stick: Why Some Ideas Survive And Others Die.* New York, NY: Random House. A great resource for understanding what makes any idea truly memorable. Not a training book, but an entertaining and relevant look at human memory.

Margulies, Nancy. (2002). *Mapping Inner Space.* Chicago, IL: Zephyr Press. Probably the best book about concept mapping and graphic organizers ever written. A "must have" if you want to include these powerful memory tools in your classes and training programs.

Margulies, Nancy; Valenza, Christine. (2005). *Visual Thinking.* Norwalk, CT: Crown House Publishing. A guide for the artistic neophyte, or for anyone beginning the process of converting words into images.

Meier, Thomas. (1999). *The Accelerated Learning Coursebuilder.* Lake Geneva, WI: The Center for Accelerated Learning. A handsomely-boxed kit of six, spiral bound books that cover all aspects of Accelerated Learning. Includes hundreds of ways to use the AL strategies. Call 262-248-7070 for ordering information. Tom Meier is the son of David Meier and the director of the European Branch of the Center for Accelerated Learning.

Millbower, Lenn. (2000). *Training With A Beat.* Sterling, VA: Stylus Publishing. An easy read that offers brain-based reasons for including music in every learning experience.

Pike, Robert. (2003, 3rd edition). *Creative Training Techniques Handbook.* Amherst, MA: HRD Press. A trainer's basic how-to book that gives practical information about training design and delivery. Bob Pike is the president of The Bob Pike Group.

Pink, Daniel. (2006, 2nd edition). *A Whole New Mind: Why Right-Brainers Will Rule The Future.* New York, NY: Riverhead Books. A new and refreshing look on the whole right/left brain continuum, with some implications for the classroom as well as the world at large.

Quinn, Clark. (2005). *Engaging Learning.* San Francisco, CA: Pfeiffer Co. More for the elearning designer, with important information about learner engagement and motivation.

Silberman, Mel. (2005, 2nd edition). *101 Ways To Make Training Active.* San Francisco, CA: Jossey-Bass/Pfeiffer. A practical and useful collection of active learning techniques.

Thiagarajan, Sivasailam. (2003). *Design Your Own Games And Activities.* San Francisco, CA: Jossey-Bass/Pfeiffer. A comprehensive collection of Thiagi's best framegames—activities that you can modify for specific content and audiences. Thiagi is the president of The Thiagi Group.

Wacker, Mary B. and Silverman, Lori L. (2003). *Stories Trainers Tell: 55 Ready-To-Use Stories To Make Training Stick.* San Francisco, CA: Jossey-Bass/Pfeiffer. Useful tools for crafting memorable stories. Includes fifty-five, ready-made stories that readers have permission to use in their own training.

Westcott, Jean and Hammond, Landau. (1997). *A Picture's Worth 1,000 Words.* San Francisco, CA: Jossey-Bass/Pfeiffer. Shows the reader how to add simple yet powerful graphics, images, cartoons, shapes, and doodles to written or printed information.

Brain Science Websites

This page contains a short list of some interesting websites (in order of usefulness), which all offer free information about the human brain and learning. In addition to the websites below, do an Internet search for any of the phrases listed in the *Web Warm-Ups* activity on page 34. You'll find lots of interesting content, some of it "need-to-know" some of it "nice-to-know," and some of it about the application of brain science to teaching, training, and learning.

www.Bowperson.com

Sharon Bowman's website. Offers dozens of free, downloadable articles, book excerpts, and activities that apply brain science to both classroom-based and elearning instruction.

For *The Six Trumps® Workshop* postcard master, table cards, and slide set, log onto Sharon's website and click on the "Articles" link; then scroll to the following links:

- ▶ *The Six Trumps® Workshop Postcard*
- ▶ *The Six Trumps® Workshop Table Cards*
- ▶ *The Six Trumps® Workshop Slide Set*

www.brainrules.net

Author John Medina's excellent website with dozens of informative ways to explore brain science.

www.jensenlearning.com

Author Eric Jensen's website. An expansive collection of products and free information supporting brain-based learning and instruction.

www.alcenter.com

The Center for Accelerated Learning. Dave Meier, Director. A comprehensive and very useful website that explores all aspects of Accelerated Learning.

www.patwolfe.com

Mind Matters Inc. Author Patricia Wolfe's website. Contains articles and other resources especially compiled for classroom educators; also offers an extensive list of neuroscientific articles.

www.brainlady.com

Author Marilee Sprenger's website with brain science articles for educators.

www.tedtalks.com/search

Ted Talks: Ideas Worth Spreading. Search for the keywords "the brain" to find a variety of unique and thought-provoking twenty-minute talks by scientists and researchers about various brain-related topics.

http://brainconnection.positscience.com/

A newsletter publication with articles submitted by professionals in many different educational and scientific fields.

www.slideshare.net/garr/brain-rules-for-presenters

Author Garr Reynolds' slide show with John Medina's brain science material.

www.presentationzen.com

Author Garr Reynolds' website and blog. Explores whole new ways of using Powerpoint® and other slide-based media to teach; includes slide shows about brain science related to visual learning.

Sharon's Books, Website, and Bio

**Find FREE excerpts of
many of Sharon's best-selling books at**

WWW.Bowperson.com

Purachase Sharon's books at

www.amazon.com

For quantity discounts call

775-749-5247

www.Bowperson.com
SBowperson@gmail.com

Bowperson Publishing & Training, Inc.
P.O. Box 564, Glenbrook, NV 89413
P/775-749-5247 • F/775-749-1891

Sharon L. Bowman, M.A.
PROFESSIONAL TRAINER & SPEAKER

- ▶ Professional speaker and international trainer
- ▶ Professional development instructor for educational institutions
- ▶ Author of seven popular training books
- ▶ President, Bowperson Publishing & Training, Inc.
- ▶ Professional Member, National Speakers Association (NSA) and American Society for Training and Development (ASTD)

Sharon turns passive listeners into active learners with her high-energy, hands-on approach to teaching, training, and learning. Her classes and seminars are practical, useful, memorable, and fun. Close to 200,000 of her popular books are now in print.

Sharon has been a professional speaker, author, teacher, and trainer for almost forty years. She works with people who want to fine-tune their instructional skills, and businesses and educational institutions that want to offer exceptional professional development programs. She designs and delivers interactive keynote and conference sessions, and customized train-the-trainer programs.

The idea is to write it so that people hear it
and it slides through the brain
and goes straight to the heart.

Maya Angelou

❑ ❑ ❑ ❑ ❑ ❑ ❑